FROM WHERE I SIT

ANYTHING AND EVERYTHING IS POSSIBLE

A Compassionate Guide for Parents and Professionals Supporting Children with Disabilities

ZULLY JF ALVARADO

Dedication

To every child who has ever been told they were "different", to those who learned to walk with metal companions, who found strength in silence, who discovered that courage isn't the absence of fear but the decision to keep moving forward despite it.

To the warriors who fight battles no one sees, who adapt and overcome not once, but every single day. To those who have transformed their pain into purpose, their struggles into strength, their limitations into launching pads for extraordinary lives.

To the children who grew up against all odds and not only survived but learned to fight the good fight, this book is your story, your truth, your triumph.

You are not broken.
You are not less than.
You are beautifully, powerfully, perfectly you.

This book stands as testimony that from where we sit, we can see farther, love deeper, and shine brighter than we ever imagined possible.

To the fighters, the adapters, the brave ones, this is for you.

Contents

PART V: LEADERSHIP FROM THE MARGINS

PART VI: DIGITAL FREEDOM AND THE FUTURE

INTRODUCTION

THE VIEW FROM HERE

From where I sit today, sunlight spilling across my desk, wheels glinting beneath me, I see possibility everywhere.

This was not always the case. There were years when my view was obscured by pain, limited by equipment, and narrowed by other people's assumptions about what my life could or should be. There were moments when the weight of metal braces felt heavier than my dreams, when crutches carried me further from belonging rather than closer to it, and when my wheelchair felt more like a prison than a passport to freedom. Looking back, I see that moment differently now; it became a doorway to everything this book explores.

But through decades of navigating the world with visible disability, I've learned something powerful: the view changes not when our circumstances change, but when we change how we see.

What This Book Is, and Isn't

This isn't a feel-good story meant to make you grateful for your own challenges. It's a deeper invitation, to understand, to reimagine, and to see disability as a wellspring of creativity and power. It is not a tale of "overcoming" disability because disability is not something to overcome.

It's part of who I am, woven into the fabric of my identity as deeply as my love for design, my passion for service, and my commitment to freedom.

Instead, this is a story about transformation, about how the very things that mark us as different, the braces, crutches, canes, and wheelchairs, can become our greatest sources of creativity, courage, and purpose. It's also a practical guide for parents, caregivers, educators, and professionals who want to understand what those experiences feel like for a child, and how to respond with empathy instead of assumption.

That realization shaped the heart of this book.

Each story in these pages reveals what it's like to grow up moving through a world designed for someone else. Each insight chapter translates those experiences into tools you can use, to raise, teach, or care for a child who uses assistive equipment with confidence and dignity.

Before we explore those insights together, let me share where they come from because the path that shaped them is as essential as the lessons themselves.

From the Margins to the Center

My journey has taken me from a dusty village in Ecuador, where doctors told my parents I wouldn't live long, to hospital ships and rehabilitation centers in the United States, to corporate boardrooms and international stages. I've designed shoes for people with hard-to-fit feet, built accessible community gardens, and created a nonprofit that's touched lives across continents. I've also learned that entrepreneurship and technology can be tools of freedom for anyone who has ever been told they don't belong.

But more than anything, this is a story about redefining what's possible and helping others do the same.

Why This Story Matters Now

We live in an age that celebrates inclusion, yet visible differences still unsettle people. Despite decades of advocacy and legislation, people with disabilities remain underrepresented in leadership, underestimated in classrooms, and too often invisible in the stories we tell about success.

For instance, even today, only a few public spaces are fully accessible, and less than 5% of media leaders identify as having a disability. Progress is happening but it's uneven, and too often invisible.

This needs to change and it starts with understanding.

When we limit anyone's potential based on how they move or what equipment they use, we all lose. The innovations that make daily life easier for everyone, curb cuts, voice recognition, touch-free technology, were born from accessibility. Inclusion is not charity; it's progress. Those of us who live at the margins have always been inventors, problem solvers, and teachers of resilience.

This book invites you to learn from that margin to see disability not as limitation, but as leadership.

How to Read This Book

From Where I Sit is organized around the evolution of my relationship with mobility equipment and, more importantly, my relationship with myself.

Each pair of chapters offers both story and strategy. Story chapters open a window into a child's lived experience with mobility. Insight chapters translate those moments into understanding you can apply whether at home, in school, or in therapy. At the end of each insight chapter, you'll find three sections: *What You Can Do Right Now, What to Watch For,* and *Key Takeaways.* Use them as practical guides for action.

You can read cover to cover or skip to the section most relevant to your child, student, or patient.

An Invitation to See Differently

Whether you are raising a child with a disability, teaching one, caring for one, or simply want to create a more inclusive world, this book offers both empathy and strategy. You'll learn to recognize the emotions behind mobility transitions, to reframe frustration as adaptation, and to use technology and community as tools for independence rather than dependence.

Most of all, you'll be invited to expand your definition of what's possible. Because from where I sit, I can tell you this: strength, creativity, and courage are limitless if we're willing to see them through a new lens. The view from here is magnificent. Let me show you what I see.

PART I

The Child's View
Discovering Difference

CHAPTER 1

BRACES AND PLAYGROUND RULES

The World Before "Different"

Before anyone told me I would need leg braces, I didn't think of myself as all that different. I knew something was not quite right, that my legs didn't hold me the way I wanted, that I had to grab onto something to stand upright. But as a child, I wasn't measuring myself against anyone's definition of "normal."

This is perhaps the most precious gift of early childhood, the time before we learn that our bodies are supposed to look and function a certain way, before we understand that there are rules about how we should move through the world, before we realize that some ways of being are considered acceptable while others are not.

We lived in the country in Ecuador, not even a village, just a dusty road with our home on one side and my uncle's house across the way. A little farther down was my grandmother's. That was our world. There were no sidewalks, no playgrounds, just dirt paths and open air. My days were spent sitting, watching, and sometimes trying. The mornings smelled of earth and milk. Roosters crowed, and the air carried the hum of insects and the sound of distant laughter. Dust rose around my feet when I tried to stand, and in that golden haze, the difference didn't yet have a name.

In that simple environment, my differences felt less pronounced. There were no stairs to struggle with, no perfectly paved surfaces that highlighted my unsteady gait, no other children running past me with the kind of easy grace I would never possess. Nature didn't judge. The dirt didn't care how I moved across it. The chickens in our yard didn't stare at my crooked steps or whisper about my struggles.

But even in that accepting landscape, my body told its own story.

This was a time when people with disabilities were largely invisible. We were institutionalized, kept at home, hidden away. Society's attitude was clear: if you couldn't walk, stand, or look a certain way, you didn't belong in public spaces. I rarely saw other wheelchair users out in the world. The message was everywhere; people like me were expected to stay out of sight.

The Vocabulary of Difference

One afternoon, I picked up a machete, heavy and sharp in my small hands, and used it almost like a walking stick. In my clumsy attempt to steady myself and move forward, the blade slipped into my right foot. Blood everywhere. I don't remember pain so much as the shock of red against the dirt.

Looking back now, I see this moment as one of my first negotiations with adaptive equipment. Even as a young child, my body instinctively understood that it needed support, assistance, something to lean against. The machete was dangerous and inappropriate, but my impulse was correct; I needed tools to help me navigate the world.

Other times, it was my left side that betrayed me, my foot dragging, my back curved from scoliosis, each step a crooked, stubborn effort. Running was not in my memory. Jumping, chasing, playing with other children; these were stories I heard, not things I lived.

But in my family, this wasn't treated as tragedy. My parents had no money for doctors, equipment, or treatments. We had a cow, we had nature, we had the rhythm of survival. I remember my father carrying me on the front bar of his bicycle to the fields, where he would milk the cow and hand me a cup, still warm and foamy. That was comforting. That was life.

This acceptance, not of limitation, but of reality, would become one of my greatest strengths. My parents didn't treat me as broken or lesser. They simply adapted. When I couldn't walk to the fields, my father carried me. When I couldn't chase the other children, they found other ways for me to be included. They were teaching me, without words, that every problem has a solution, and that love adapts.

The Journey to "Help"

When the decision was made that I needed medical treatment, it wasn't explained to me in ways I could understand. I was taken to a hospital ship that had docked for a medical mission in Ecuador. The doctors examined me, talked among themselves, and made arrangements. I didn't know that they had told my family I was malnourished and unlikely to live a long life without help. I didn't know they'd recommended I be brought to the United States for care.

I only knew I was leaving home.

This is where many stories of childhood disability begin, with adults making decisions that children don't understand, using words like "help" and "treatment" that sound positive but often feel frightening.

The medical model of disability teaches us to see disability as a problem located in the person, as something broken that needs to be fixed. It focuses on cure, correction, and control. The child becomes a project, and success is defined by how closely they resemble the "normal" body.

But there's another way to see it. The social model shifts the focus from fixing the child to fixing the environment. It asks different questions: How can we change the systems, spaces, and expectations around this child so they can participate fully? What if the problem isn't in the body, but in the barriers?

When we start from that perspective, "help" takes on a new meaning. It's no longer about normalizing the child; it's about helping them thrive exactly as they are.

I wouldn't understand this distinction for decades. At the time, I simply knew that I was being separated from everything familiar, carried toward something unknown, placed in the hands of strangers who spoke a different language and saw my body through the lens of deficit rather than possibility.

First Contact with the Medical System

In the U.S., I was taken to Shriners Hospital. Everything there was strange: the language, the smells, the bright white lights. I remember lying under a heavy piece of equipment during an X-ray, feeling like I was about to be crushed. In my mind, I wasn't a patient; I was a cucaracha, a cockroach under a shoe.

This image still haunts me, not because it was traumatic, but because it was accurate. The medical system, for all its good intentions, often treats children with disabilities like specimens to be studied rather than human beings to be understood. We are poked, prodded, measured, and assessed. We are talked about in our presence as though we cannot hear or understand. We are reduced to diagnoses, prognoses, and treatment plans.

I didn't understand the purpose of the tests, the measuring, the endless Friday afternoons of therapy. No one explained.

As a child, I didn't have words for it. I only knew it felt like being invisible.

This lack of explanation, this assumption that children don't need to understand what's being done to their own bodies, is one of the most damaging aspects of pediatric medical care. When we don't help children understand their own conditions, when we don't involve them in decisions about their own bodies, when we don't teach them to advocate for themselves, we create adults who feel disconnected from their own experience, who struggle to articulate their needs, who see themselves as passive recipients of care rather than active participants in their own lives.

The Promise of Steel

I kept hearing a word in Spanish, fierro, steel. They said I would be wearing a brace. I imagined something solid, something that would straighten me out, fix my legs, make them strong. I thought maybe it would give me muscles, or make my thinner leg match the thicker one.

This is the seductive promise of medical intervention. That the right equipment, the right surgery, the right therapy will make us "normal." As children, we absorb this message eagerly. We want to be fixed. We want to fit in. We want our bodies to work the way other bodies work.

But what no one tells you is that adaptive equipment doesn't make you normal. It makes you functional. There's a crucial difference. Normal suggests conformity to a standard. Functional suggests the ability to do what you need to do. Normal is about appearance. Functional is about capability. Normal is about fitting in. Functional is about living fully.

I didn't know what my brace would really be like until the day it arrived.

I remember waiting for the brace with a strange mix of excitement and dread, imagining how it might transform me. In my child's mind, steel meant power, it meant I would finally stand tall, finally move like everyone else. I couldn't yet imagine that the thing I longed for would also become the heaviest part of me.

The Reality of Steel

Two long metal bars, leather straps, a hinge at the ankle. The shoes, drilled into the bars, mismatched sizes because one foot was smaller than the other, were black and white, stiff, and heavy. They were the only shoes I was allowed to wear.

Looking at my brace for the first time, I experienced what many children with disabilities come to know intimately: the gap between promise and reality. This device was not going to make me normal. It was not going to give me muscles or straighten my spine or help me run with the other children.

It was simply going to help me stand.

But even that limited goal came with a price. The leather straps rubbed against my knees, leaving raw blisters. I tried wrapping cotton and cloth around the sore spots, pulling thick socks over my skin to soften the scrape. Nothing worked for long. The brace was cold and unyielding, especially in the Midwest winters. The metal froze against my skin, and every step felt heavier.

This is the hidden curriculum of adaptive equipment: the lessons no one teaches you about pain management, skin care, the daily negotiations between function and comfort. You learn to live with discomfort. You learn to hide it. You learn that the cost of mobility is constant, low-level pain, and that complaining about it marks you as ungrateful.

The hinge at the ankle squeaked and clicked so loudly I couldn't move quietly anywhere. Hide-and-seek was impossible; they could hear me coming before they saw me. This was my first introduction to the loss of invisibility that comes with visible disability. Before the brace, I could choose when to reveal my differences. After the brace, they announced themselves with every step.

The Exhaustion of Being Different

Wearing the brace was exhausting. I counted the hours until bedtime, when I could finally take it off. I learned to tolerate the weight, but never what came with it. At school and in the neighborhood, the brace made me different in ways I couldn't hide.

This exhaustion is something that people without disabilities rarely understand. It's not just the physical effort of moving with equipment; though that is real and significant. It's the emotional and psychological effort of being constantly visible, constantly explaining, constantly managing other people's reactions to your body.

The other kids ran, jumped rope, and played tag. I stood at the edges, trying to join in, but always being left behind. This is where I first learned about social geography: how physical spaces and social activities are designed around certain assumptions about how bodies work.

Playgrounds are particularly revealing in this regard. They are spaces designed for running, climbing, swinging, jumping, all activities that assume a certain kind of physical capability. When your body doesn't work that way, playgrounds become landscapes of exclusion, reminders of everything you can't do rather than celebrations of what you can.

Once, during recess, a teacher asked me to 'sit out' because she worried I might fall. The other children didn't look at me cruelly. They just forgot I was there. That quiet forgetting hurt more than any teasing could.

But standing at the edges taught me something valuable: the power of observation. While other children were busy playing, I was learning to watch, to analyze, to understand group dynamics and social patterns. I was developing skills that would serve me well in leadership roles later in life, the ability to assess situations, to see what others miss, to understand systems from the outside.

The Politics of Clothing

Just like braces or crutches, clothes become part of how others see you and how you learn to see yourself. The politics of clothing is really about who gets to decide what "normal" looks like.

Clothes were a constant battle. I either wore heavy slacks to hide the brace or pulled it over my pants, which looked awkward and unfashionable, even for a child.

This may seem like a small concern, but fashion and self-expression are crucial parts of identity development, especially for young people. When your clothing choices are limited by your equipment, when you can't wear what your peers are wearing, when every outfit is a negotiation between function and style, you learn early that your body shapes your options in ways that other bodies don't.

This experience would later influence my decision to become a fashion designer, specializing in clothing and footwear for people with disabilities. I understood, from personal experience, the frustration of not being able to express yourself through what you wear, the challenge of finding clothes that accommodate equipment, the importance of feeling attractive and stylish regardless of your physical needs.

But as a child, I simply felt the sting of being marked as different. Fashion was one more area where my disability set me apart, one more reminder that I didn't fit into the world as it was designed.

The Silence of Survival

I felt what any child would feel, but I didn't show my feelings openly. That silence, painful as it was, also taught me to listen to hear what others left unsaid, to recognize when someone was hiding their own pain. I was living with a family that wasn't my own, people who had power of attorney over me while I was in the U.S. I didn't want to cause trouble or risk losing the little stability I had. So I swallowed the tears, smiled when expected, and carried the weight of the brace and of being different.

This is perhaps the most damaging lesson that children with disabilities learn: that our emotional needs are secondary to other people's comfort. We learn not to complain, not to cry, not to express frustration or sadness about our circumstances. We learn that gratitude is expected, even when we're struggling. We learn that being "good patients" and "inspirational figures" is more important than being authentic human beings with complex feelings.

The pressure to be grateful is particularly intense for children whose medical care is provided through charity or public programs. There's an implicit message that you should be thankful for what you're given, that questioning or critiquing the system that "helps" you is ungrateful, that your role is to be a success story rather than a real person.

But what happens to all those swallowed tears? What happens to all that unexpressed frustration? Where does all that authentic emotion go when it's not allowed to be expressed?

For many of us, it turns inward. It becomes depression, anxiety, a sense of disconnection from our own experience. Or it explodes outward in unexpected ways in rebellion, in anger, in choices that seem to contradict our "inspirational" image.

Learning to reclaim our right to our own emotions, to express frustration and sadness and anger about the real challenges we face, is one of the most important parts of developing a healthy relationship with disability. It's not about becoming bitter or negative; it's about becoming whole.

For a long time, that silence felt like weakness. But over time, I began to see it differently, not as absence, but as incubation. Beneath the quiet, something strong was forming: the will to adapt, the courage to endure, the beginnings of resilience.

The Seeds of Resilience

Despite all the challenges, those early years with leg braces taught me skills that would serve me for the rest of my life. I learned problem-solving: how to navigate stairs, how to manage pain, how to modify activities so I could participate. I learned creativity: how to play games differently, how to find ways to belong even when I couldn't do what everyone else was doing.

Most importantly, I learned that adaptation is possible. My body had to work differently, so I learned to work differently. My social experience was different, so I learned to create different kinds of connections. My challenges were unique, so I learned to develop unique solutions.

These are the hidden gifts of childhood disability, not inspiration about "overcoming" challenges, but real skills that emerge from real experience. Problem-solving. Creativity. Adaptability. Resilience. Empathy. The ability to see systems from multiple perspectives. The capacity to find alternatives when the obvious path is blocked.

Children with disabilities often grow up to be innovative adults precisely because we've had to innovate from the beginning. We've had to find ways around obstacles, develop creative solutions, and think outside conventional frameworks. These are valuable skills in any context, but they're particularly valuable in leadership, entrepreneurship, and social change work.

The question is not whether children with disabilities develop resilience; we have no choice but to develop it. The question is whether the adults around us recognize and nurture that resilience, whether they help us see our adaptations as strengths rather than compensations, whether they support us in developing our unique gifts rather than trying to make us as "normal" as possible.

For adult readers, especially parents, it's worth pausing here to consider what this journey looks like from a child's perspective. The medical interventions that seem like obvious solutions to you may feel like violations to your child. The equipment that represents progress to you may represent loss to them. The goals you have for their body may not align with their experience of living in that body. This doesn't mean the interventions are wrong; it means they need to be accompanied by emotional support, honest communication, and space for the child's authentic feelings.

From my first wobbly steps in leg braces, I was learning that the goal was not to be like everyone else. The goal was to be fully myself, to find ways to live and move and connect that honored both my capabilities and my limitations, to discover that being different wasn't a problem to be solved but a reality to be embraced.

The braces were heavy, uncomfortable, and limiting. But they were also my first teachers in the art of adaptation, my first introduction to the possibility that equipment could be a tool of freedom rather than a symbol of limitation. They taught me the playground rules and how to rewrite them. The goal was never to fit in, but to learn when and how to change the game itself.

CHAPTER 2

WHAT PARENTS SHOULD KNOW ABOUT BRACES

When a child first receives an assistive device, a brace, splint, or any piece of adaptive equipment, they're being introduced to far more than a medical intervention. They're beginning a lifelong conversation with their own body. How adults handle this introduction can turn that conversation into one of empowerment or one of shame. This chapter explores how to ensure it's the former.

The Psychology Behind the Equipment

By the time a child is five, they've already started to notice how people's bodies look and move and they begin forming ideas about what's "normal." That's why the early years are such an important window. The way adults talk about equipment during this stage can either build confidence or plant seeds of shame.

When a child receives their first brace, they're at a crucial stage of identity formation. For young children (ages 3-6), this is when they're learning to assert themselves and explore what they can do. The introduction of adaptive equipment during this sensitive period can either support healthy confidence or inadvertently create shame about their bodies.

Research shows that children's adjustment to assistive devices is heavily influenced by their parents' and caregivers' attitudes. When adults frame equipment as a tool for freedom rather than a symbol of limitation, children are more likely to develop positive associations with their devices. Conversely, when adults express sadness, pity, or excessive concern about equipment, children internalize the message that something is fundamentally wrong with them.

For instance, one mother described her daughter's brace as her 'superhero legs,' emphasizing strength and mobility. Another parent focused on what her son couldn't do without it. Both children wore similar equipment but one saw it as power, the other as punishment.

A parent's attitude isn't just emotional; it becomes linguistic. The way you explain your child's equipment, the tone you use, and the story you tell about why it exists all shape how they'll understand their body.

What adults sometimes overlook is that a brace isn't just a device; it becomes part of a child's daily sensory world. Children make sense of their bodies through touch, movement, and pattern. When something new changes the way they walk, sit, or play, they naturally try to understand what it means. If they aren't given words or explanations, they fill in the blanks themselves and young children tend to personalize everything.

A child might quietly wonder, *"Did I do something wrong?"* or *"Why is my body different from my friends' bodies?"* Without guidance, these questions turn into private conclusions that may follow them well into adulthood.

But when children *do* understand their equipment, when they hear, "This is here to help your body work its best," or "Your brace gives your muscles support while you grow", the device becomes less mysterious. Their nervous system relaxes. Their imagination shifts from fear to curiosity. They begin to see the brace as something working *with* them instead of something happening *to* them.

This cognitive clarity directly supports healthy identity formation. Children build their sense of self through meaning-making, and a clear, positive narrative about their equipment gives them a stable foundation to understand their difference without shame.

Explanation, therefore, isn't a side note; it's the emotional blueprint for how your child will interpret their difference.

Why Explanation Matters More Than You Think

One of the most significant gaps in pediatric orthopedic care is the failure to include children in age-appropriate conversations about their own bodies and equipment. Studies show that fewer than 30% of children receiving assistive devices report receiving adequate explanations about why they need the equipment, how it works, or what to expect.

This lack of explanation leaves children without the words or frameworks to understand their own experience. Without a coherent story about their disability and their equipment, children construct their own narratives, often incorporating the confused or pitying reactions they observe in others.

Children are also astute observers of social cues. They notice when adults hesitate before mentioning the brace, when strangers stare, or when a teacher over-assists out of uncertainty. Their bodies become mirrors reflecting the reactions of the people around them.

When a child understands *why* they wear equipment, it gives them language to interpret these moments with clarity rather than confusion. A four-year-old who says proudly, "This helps my legs stay strong when I run," is processing a social reaction with confidence instead of fear. That single sentence can keep a child from internalizing the subtle shame that often comes from other people's discomfort.

Children need a "disability narrative" early in life: a positive, accurate story about their body that acknowledges both challenges and capabilities. This narrative doesn't sugarcoat difficulties or promise unrealistic outcomes. Instead, it provides context, normalizes adaptation, and emphasizes that different bodies require different tools.

How to Talk to Children About Braces

The language adults use with children about disability shapes their self-concept profoundly. The key principle is this: the problem is not the child's body, but the world's failure to accommodate diverse bodies.

Consider these two approaches:

Avoid This Approach: "Your legs don't work the way they should, so we're going to fix them with this brace. If you wear it every day, maybe someday you won't need it anymore."

Try This Instead: "Your legs work differently than some people's legs, so you need special equipment to help you do the things you want to do. Lots of people use different kinds of equipment to help their bodies work best."

The first approach centers on what's "wrong" and creates false hope of a cure. The second acknowledges difference without making it a defect and sets realistic expectations.

Effective Communication Includes:

Remember that children don't just hear your words, they watch your face and your body language. If you introduce the brace with tension in your shoulders or worry in your voice, children sense that something is "off." If you present it with calm interest, even delight, they absorb that emotional tone instead.

Many children actually respond with excitement when adults frame the equipment as a new tool, a new adventure, or something special that will help them participate more fully in the world. Your energy becomes their first teacher.

Concrete, sensory-based explanations: "The brace helps your leg stay strong and straight, like how a trellis helps a plant grow tall."

Acknowledgment of discomfort: "The straps might feel tight at first, and that's okay to talk about. We'll work together to make it as comfortable as possible."

Emphasis on function, not normalization: "This brace helps you stand and walk so you can play and explore" rather than "This will make your legs more normal."

Opportunities for choice and agency: Allowing children to choose colors, decorations, or when (within medical guidelines) they wear their equipment gives them a sense of control.

Here's how that can sound in real life:

"You might say, 'This brace is going to help your leg stay steady when you walk. It might feel tight at first, like a hug around your leg. Let's see what kind of games we can still play together with it on.' The goal isn't perfection, it's connection."

These small, sensory-rich conversations help children see their equipment not as correction, but as collaboration, with both their body and the adults who support them.

Equipment as Companion, Not Punishment

Instead of presenting braces as medical interventions imposed by authority figures, try helping children see their equipment as a partner in their daily adventures. This might involve:

- Naming the equipment (many children naturally do this).
- Creating "equipment care" rituals that give children responsibility.
- Connecting with other children who use similar equipment.
- Reading books featuring characters with disabilities and adaptive equipment.
- Celebrating "firsts" accomplished with equipment, not despite it.

Children often form emotional attachments to objects that support them, blankets, toys, stuffed animals. Adaptive equipment, though more functional than cuddly, can become emotionally meaningful in similar ways. A brace they wear during big achievements, first steps, first time climbing onto a playground structure, first time keeping up with a sibling, becomes woven into the story they tell themselves about what they're capable of.

When adults honor these emotional connections, the equipment becomes less clinical and more personal. A child might say, "My brace helped me do that," and feel genuine pride. That shift, from device as punishment to device as partner, is a powerful developmental milestone.

What the Medical System Often Gets Wrong

The medical approach to childhood disability has historically focused on bringing children as close to "normal" function as possible. While functional improvement is certainly valuable, an exclusive focus on normalization can have unintended psychological consequences.

Studies following children who received intensive early intervention for physical disabilities found that those whose treatment emphasized functional adaptation, learning to accomplish tasks in whatever way worked for their bodies, reported higher self-esteem and life satisfaction than those whose treatment emphasized normalization, achieving skills in "typical" ways.

The problem with the fixing paradigm is that it positions the child's natural body as defective and the goal as becoming less disabled. This sets up a lifelong internal conflict: if success means minimizing disability, then the persistence of disability, which is often unavoidable, feels like failure.

Common Medical Professional Mistakes:

Talking over the child: Discussing treatment plans, prognosis, and equipment exclusively with parents while the child is present but excluded from the conversation.

Using fear-based motivation: "If you don't wear your brace, your legs will get worse" creates anxiety rather than understanding.

Minimizing the child's experience: "It doesn't hurt that much" or "You'll get used to it" dismisses legitimate discomfort and teaches children not to trust their own perceptions.

Promising unrealistic outcomes: Suggesting that perfect compliance with equipment use will result in "normal" function creates a setup for disappointment and self-blame.

Ignoring the social and emotional dimensions: Focusing exclusively on biomechanics while neglecting the child's emotional experience, peer relationships, and identity development.

If a child's medical team is making these mistakes, parents and caregivers have the right to advocate for a more holistic approach, one that treats the child as a whole person and addresses functional goals within the context of their actual life, not just clinical measures.

Children rarely think in medical terms, they think in lived terms: *Can I play? Can I keep up? Can I try what my friends are trying?* When medical providers overlook this, they unintentionally miss the emotional reality of childhood. A brace that allows a child to join a game of tag matters just as much as and sometimes more than a degree of corrected alignment.

When treatment supports the child's lived experiences, the equipment becomes not just a health intervention but a doorway back into childhood itself.

Parents can't always change the medical system, but they can shape how their child experiences it. By asking questions, modeling curiosity, and insisting that the child be included, you transform clinical encounters into moments of empowerment.

Teaching Self-Advocacy From the Start

One of the most valuable skills adults can teach children who use adaptive equipment is self-advocacy, the ability to identify their needs, communicate them clearly, and request appropriate accommodations. This skill development should begin as soon as children start using equipment.

Early Self-Advocacy by Age:

For preschool-age children (3-5 years):

- Teaching simple scripts: "My brace helps me walk" or "I need help with the stairs".

- Role-playing common scenarios (answering questions about equipment, asking for assistance).
- Praising attempts to communicate needs, even if imperfectly expressed.

For early elementary age (6-8 years):

- Helping children explain their equipment to peers in their own words.
- Teaching them to identify when equipment needs adjustment.
- Supporting them in making simple decisions about equipment use within medical guidelines.

For older elementary age (9-12 years):

- Involving children in appointments and encouraging them to ask questions.
- Teaching problem-solving frameworks for accessibility challenges.
- Connecting them with disability communities and role models.

The Power of Play

My background in child development has taught me one truth that cannot be overstated: play is everything. Jean Piaget famously argued that play is not just a leisure activity; it is the very architecture through which children build their understanding of the world. Through play, children test hypotheses, explore cause and effect, and gain sensory and spatial mastery over their environment.

When children move, climb, balance, crawl, and explore, they are continuously wiring neurological pathways that support coordination, problem-solving, language, emotional regulation, and social understanding. These aren't optional "extras" in childhood development; they are the core work of growing up.

Play is children's primary method of processing experiences and emotions. Yet we are living in a time when children, across all abilities, aren't playing nearly enough. Screens have replaced playgrounds, structured activities have replaced open-ended exploration, and many families lack access to safe outdoor environments. For children with disabilities, these barriers multiply. Mobility challenges, overprotectiveness, inaccessible playgrounds, and limited therapeutic guidance often mean these children get even *less* physical play than their peers.

This lack of movement has developmental consequences. Children learn through their bodies. The less they move, the harder it becomes for them to develop motor planning, sensory organization, spatial awareness, and the confidence that comes from mastering their own physical abilities.

For children with adaptive equipment, play serves crucial functions:

- **Mastery**: Practicing skills and movements that feel challenging in real life.
- **Expression**: Working through feelings about equipment, medical experiences, and social reactions.
- **Integration**: Incorporating equipment into their self-concept through imaginative play.
- **Connection**: Finding ways to play with peers despite physical differences.

But these four functions only scratch the surface. Play is a whole-body developmental system, fueling growth across every domain:

Motor Skills: Physical play strengthens balance, coordination, core stability, and endurance. Children with braces, walkers, or wheelchairs need even more opportunities to move freely so they can experiment with how their equipment works in real-world environments, not just clinical ones. A child who practices climbing with a brace is developing not only muscle control but also the confidence to test their limits safely.

Sensory Awareness: Through tactile, vestibular, and proprioceptive input, children learn where their body is in space. Piaget understood that sensory-motor experiences form the base layer for all higher-level thinking. When a child rolls down a hill, feels the vibration of a swing, or experiments with how their brace changes their movement, they're building a map of their own body and that map becomes the foundation for planning, coordination, and emotional regulation.

Imagination & Narrative Development: Play lets children rewrite the story of their equipment. A walker becomes a spaceship console. A brace becomes a knight's armor. A wheelchair becomes a racing chariot. Children are natural meaning-makers, and imaginative play allows them to transform something adults might frame as "medical" into something powerful, heroic, or exciting.

Emotional Development: In play, children rehearse courage, frustration, problem-solving, and resilience. When they pretend their brace is a tool or a superpower, they're processing real emotions about their disability in a safe, symbolic space. This develops emotional flexibility, an essential protective factor throughout life.

Adults Can Support Therapeutic Play By:

- Providing dolls or action figures with adaptive equipment.
- Creating play scenarios that mirror the child's experiences (doctor visits, playground challenges).
- Following the child's lead in how they incorporate disability into their play narratives.
- Avoiding the temptation to "correct" play that seems negative (children often work through difficult emotions by playing them out).

Why Adult Support Matters

Adults often underestimate how deeply children are shaped by play environments. When children with disabilities are given fewer opportunities to climb, run, jump, or take physical risks, they internalize the idea that their bodies are fragile or limited. Supporting safe, joyful physical play where children can challenge themselves without fear builds a positive, resilient body identity.

Moreover, when adults show genuine curiosity ("What does your brace help you do on the slide?") rather than anxiety ("Be careful!"), children feel permission to explore and experiment.

Play often reveals what words can't. For many children, play becomes the place where they test out new identities: the brave explorer with a supportive leg brace, the superhero whose powers come from adaptive tools, the inventor who upgrades their gear to overcome obstacles. These storylines help children integrate the equipment into their developing sense of self without shame.

Unfortunately, children with disabilities often receive the least access to this imaginative and physical world. Well-meaning adults may keep them seated to avoid falls, limit their movement to carpeted or "safe" areas, or rely heavily on structured therapy instead of unstructured exploration.

But therapy alone cannot replace play. Therapy teaches skills; play teaches identity, agency, and the belief that "My body can do things. My body is allowed to try."

When children are not given enough space to move, experiment, build, tumble, and explore, they lose critical opportunities for both physical and emotional growth. And most importantly: they lose opportunities to discover joy in their own bodies.

When adults join this play without directing it, they're quietly reinforcing the message: *Your equipment is part of you, and that's okay. More than okay, it's powerful.*

In the make-believe worlds children build, you can glimpse how they're learning to live with difference and sometimes, how they're teaching you to see it.

Play is not extra. It is not optional. It is not a luxury squeezed in after appointments and routines. Play is the developmental engine of childhood, especially for children whose bodies work differently.

When we ensure that children with disabilities have rich, physical, imaginative play, we're not just supporting their therapy goals. We're supporting their whole identity. We are helping them build confidence, agency, problem-solving skills, emotional resilience, sensory organization, and a story about themselves that says:

"I am strong. I am capable. I am allowed to take up space in the world."

That is the true power of play.

Validating All the Feelings

Children with disabilities often receive implicit messages that their feelings about their experiences don't matter as much as being "brave" or "grateful." Developing emotional literacy, the ability to identify, understand, and express feelings, is crucial for long-term psychological health.

Strategies for Building Emotional Literacy:

- **Use feeling words regularly:** "I notice you seem frustrated with your brace today. Frustration is okay."

- **Validate difficult emotions:** "It makes sense that you feel sad when you can't do everything the other kids do."
- **Distinguish between feelings and facts:** "You feel like everyone is staring at you. Let's talk about what's actually happening and how we can help you feel more comfortable."
- **Create safe outlets for negative emotions:** journaling, art, physical activity adapted to their abilities.
- **Model emotional honesty:** Share (age-appropriately) when you feel frustrated, sad, or challenged.

Children with disabilities often learn to suppress their authentic feelings to avoid being seen as ungrateful or difficult. The job of caring adults is to create space for all their emotions, the hard ones, the messy ones, the ones that don't fit the "inspirational" narrative others may expect.

When children learn that all their feelings are valid, they also learn that all their experiences have meaning. And that's where the real learning begins, understanding not just what a brace does, but what it teaches.

When children understand the purpose of their device, it also becomes easier for them to articulate how it makes them feel. A child who knows "my brace helps my muscles stay strong" can say, "It hurts today" or "I don't like how tight it is," without believing that they themselves are the problem. Understanding the equipment acts as emotional scaffolding; it creates safety around expressing difficult experiences.

What a Brace Really Teaches

The ultimate lesson of early adaptive equipment is not about biomechanics; it's about meaning-making. When children grow up understanding why they use equipment, they learn early that their body is something they can collaborate with, not something they must hide or apologize for. This is a profound developmental gift. It protects them from internalizing stigma, equips them to advocate for themselves, and allows them to grow into teenagers and adults who see adaptation as strength, a natural part of being human.

Understanding creates dignity. And dignity, more than anything, fosters resilience.

A brace doesn't just affect how a child moves through physical space; it affects how they move through social space, how they understand their identity, and how they construct narratives about their possibilities.

When adults approach braces and other early equipment thoughtfully, with clear communication, emotional participation, and an emphasis on function rather than normalization, they teach children that:

- Their body is worthy of respect exactly as it is.
- Different doesn't mean defective.
- Adaptation is a form of intelligence, not defeat.
- Equipment is a tool for freedom, not a symbol of limitation.
- They have agency in their own lives, even when they need support.

These lessons, learned in early childhood, become the foundation for a lifetime of healthy disability identity, effective self-advocacy, and the confidence to pursue ambitious goals.

The child who learns to see their brace as a partner rather than a prison grows into an adult who reshapes the world itself. Because function isn't just freedom, it's the beginning of possibility.

Toolkit: What Adults Can Do Right Now

Understanding is powerful, but action transforms understanding into freedom. The following tools will help you translate these ideas into daily practice.

What You Can Do Right Now:

Explain what the brace does using simple, child-friendly language that emphasizes what it helps your child do, not what it "fixes."

Invite your child to personalize the brace with stickers, colors, or decorations so it feels like theirs, not something imposed on them.

Model calm confidence when others ask questions or stare; your composure becomes the internal script your child will carry.

Connect with other families whose children use similar equipment so your child sees they're not alone and can learn from shared experiences.

Create small rituals around equipment care, like cleaning, decorating, or checking comfort, to give your child a sense of ownership and routine.

Read books together that feature characters with disabilities or adaptive equipment, helping normalize difference and build representation.

Practice short, playful responses to common peer questions ("What's that?" or "Why do you wear that?") so your child feels prepared rather than self-conscious.

Involve your child in medical appointments at an age-appropriate level. Ask, "How does this feel?" or "Which color do you like best?" to show their opinions matter.

Daily Habits That Help:

Empowerment doesn't happen through big moments. It's built into daily routines. Here are a few simple habits that can make a lasting difference:

- **Name the wins.** Celebrate small successes: each day your child uses their brace with confidence or comfort is progress worth noticing.
- **Check for comfort.** Ask daily, "How does your brace feel today?" and listen closely to the answer. This small question reinforces agency and trust.
- **Use reflective praise.** Replace "good job" with "You looked strong climbing those steps today" or "You figured out a new way to play!" language that builds internal confidence rather than compliance.
- **Model flexibility.** If your child struggles with discomfort or fatigue, validate it and adjust plans when possible. Adaptation itself is a form of resilience.
- **End the day with affirmation.** A simple reminder "Your body works hard, and that's something to be proud of" helps children associate their equipment with dignity and effort, not frustration.

These daily actions, though small, create a rhythm of confidence and care that supports both the child's comfort and their growing sense of independence.

What to Watch For:

It's natural for children to need time to adjust to new equipment. Some discomfort, frustration, or hesitation is expected. But if you notice these reactions persisting beyond a few weeks or intensifying it may signal the need for additional support from your child's medical or emotional care team. Use this list as a gentle guide, not a diagnostic tool.

- **Shame or secrecy about the equipment.** Hiding it, refusing to wear it, or saying they're "bad" or "broken." → This can indicate that the child is internalizing negative messages about their body or identity.
- **Persistent physical discomfort.** Pain, blisters, or skin breakdown that doesn't improve with adjustments. → Suggests the brace or device needs refitting, or that pain is being minimized.
- **Fatigue that seems disproportionate to activity level**. → May point to the brace being too heavy, poorly aligned, or causing unnecessary strain.
- **Social withdrawal from peers or activities they previously enjoyed.** → Can signal embarrassment, anxiety, or feeling "different" in social spaces.
- **Behavioral changes like irritability, anger, or sadness.** → May reflect frustration or emotional fatigue from constantly managing visibility and difference.
- **Sleep disruption or anxiety related to equipment.** → Often connected to pain, sensory discomfort, or fear of negative attention.
- **Regression in previously developed confidence or skills.** → Indicates the need to rebuild self-assurance through positive reinforcement and communication.

If you notice one or more of these patterns, don't assume your child is simply "resisting." Instead, see it as information, a signal that something needs adjustment, whether physical, emotional, or social. Collaboration between parents, therapists, and medical providers can make all the difference.

How to Keep Perspective:

Remember, no parent gets this perfectly right, and perfection isn't the goal. What matters most is presence, not performance. Some days will feel easy, and others will bring frustration, fatigue, or worry. All of it is part of the journey.

When you model self-compassion, your child learns it too. They watch how you respond to setbacks, to moments of doubt, to the need for rest. In those quiet, imperfect moments, you're teaching them something far more powerful than perseverance; you're teaching them that worth isn't conditional on progress.

When things feel hard, take a deep breath and remind yourself: progress with adaptive equipment is rarely linear. What looks like struggle one week often becomes strength the next. Trust the process, keep the conversation open, and remember that love and understanding are as therapeutic as any brace, tool, or intervention.

Key Takeaway:

Function is freedom, and freedom begins with how you tell the story. When you frame a brace as a bridge, not a barrier, you open a lifetime of possibility.

PART II
The Adolescent's Journey Between Visibility and Belonging

CHAPTER 3

GRADUATING TO CRUTCHES

When Freedom Feels Like Another Prison

The Surgery That Changed Everything

When the day came to move from a brace to crutches, it didn't feel like freedom; it felt like another transition my body hadn't asked for. I had been told the surgery would help, that it would make my leg look more "normal." But no one explained that "normal" meant *for* them, not for me.

The procedure was described as "cosmetic," a word that still catches in my throat. It suggested that my body was an aesthetic project, something to be reshaped for appearance rather than supported for function. My leg had worked in its own way, imperfect by medical standards, but perfectly mine.

That's the quiet pressure that follows many children with visible disabilities: the push to appear less different so others can feel more comfortable. The surgery didn't promise better movement or less pain. It promised better optics. And in chasing that illusion, I ended up with more scars, both physical and emotional.

But my body did not react as the doctors had hoped. What had been described as cosmetic possibility ended in disappointment, and with it came the introduction of wooden crutches.

Looking back, I can see that this was my first real lesson in the difference between medical hope and realistic expectations. The medical system is built on the promise of improvement, of progress, of solutions. But sometimes the "solution" creates new problems. Sometimes the "improvement" is a step backward. Sometimes the promise of looking normal leads to functioning less effectively.

For parents watching a child go through a transition like this, the gap between what was promised and what actually happens can be devastating. You want so badly to help, to fix, to make things better. But sometimes the interventions meant to help actually create new challenges and your child has to live with the consequences while you grapple with whether you made the right choice.

The Weight of Wooden Hope

At first, I thought crutches might bring relief. No more leather straps rubbing against my knees. No more steel bars clinking with every step. But I quickly discovered that crutches brought their own kind of pain.

The wood felt rough under my hands, the metal tips clicking sharply against tile floors. Every step echoed louder than I wanted it to, each thud announcing my difference before I could. The blisters just moved, this time to my armpits and shoulders. The fatigue shifted too. Instead of straining my hips and legs, I now had to lift my entire body weight with arms and shoulders that weren't built for that kind of labor.

One day in gym class, my crutches slipped on the polished floor and clattered like drumsticks across the room. For a second, everyone froze; then I laughed first. It was easier to make a joke of the noise than to explain the weight behind it. Humor became another kind of balance.

This is the hidden reality of adaptive equipment: there is no perfect solution. Every device solves some problems while creating others. The goal is not to find equipment that eliminates all challenges; such equipment doesn't exist. The goal is to find equipment that gives you the most function with the least cost, that enables you to do what matters most to you.

Every step was an effort. Every day was exhausting. But this exhaustion taught me something important about energy management, a skill that would serve me well in all areas of life. When you have limited physical resources, you learn to prioritize. You learn to save your energy for what matters most. You learn to be strategic about when and how you expend effort.

As my body adjusted to the mechanics of movement, my mind struggled with another kind of weight: the gaze of others. The pain of blisters was easier to treat than the sting of being seen. Crutches didn't just change how I moved; they changed how the world looked back at me.

The Visibility Problem

And there was something else: crutches were harder to hide. With braces, I could wear slacks, heavy fabric to disguise the metal beneath. But with crutches, they were out in front for everyone to see. They drew attention before I even entered a room.

People stared. People asked. People assumed.

Once, a classmate whispered, "How long till you're better?" and I didn't know how to answer. Better than what? The question wasn't cruel; it was simply built on the assumption that my difference was temporary.

Unlike braces, which signaled a permanent difference, crutches carried a different kind of social meaning. People looked at me and thought, "She must have broken something... she'll get better soon." I could sense the questions in their eyes: What happened? How did she hurt herself?

Crutches suggested accidents, injury, or something temporary. There was an easy answer to offer; I had surgery; but inside I knew the truth. This wasn't temporary. And that made the crutches feel like a disguise, one that confused others but didn't free me from anything.

Once, in the grocery store, a woman stopped me in the aisle and said, "You'll be running around again in no time!" Her tone was cheerful, certain, and kind in that well-meaning way that still stung. I smiled and nodded, because explaining the permanence of difference felt heavier than carrying the crutches themselves. I learned early that people prefer happy endings, even when they aren't true.

Navigating New Territories

School on crutches was a new battle. Carrying books and supplies while balancing was nearly impossible. A backpack threw me off balance. Bags in my hands made my crutches trip me.

Every door was a challenge; this was before automatic door openers existed. Every staircase was an obstacle, long, gasping climbs, sometimes on hands and knees, sometimes with crutches tucked awkwardly under one arm while I crawled.

I remember once a classmate ran ahead to open a door for me, then let it slam shut before I reached it. She hadn't meant to be cruel; she just didn't realize how long it took me to get there. By the time I caught up, the laughter that followed wasn't about me, but it still echoed that way. Moments like that taught me the difference between *intention* and *impact* long before I had the words for it.

These daily negotiations with the physical environment taught me problem-solving skills that I didn't even realize I was developing. How do you carry a lunch tray when both hands are occupied with crutches? How do you take notes when you need your arms for support? How do you participate in group activities when the space isn't designed for your kind of movement?

Every day required innovation. Every activity required adaptation. I was learning to be an inventor, an engineer, a creative problem-solver not because I chose to, but because I had to.

I remember trying to carry a lunch tray once, balancing it on one crutch like a circus act, praying it wouldn't tip. A teacher rushed over, panicked, and insisted I let her help. I wanted to say, "I've got this," but what I really meant was, "Please don't make me the story of your good deed today."

This is one of the hidden gifts of disability: it forces you to become resourceful. When the world isn't designed for you, you have to redesign it. When systems don't include you, you have to create inclusion. When solutions don't exist, you have to invent them.

Winter's Harsh Lessons

Winter was the hardest. Snow, ice, wind, and gray skies made every morning feel like a trial. I remember trudging through snow with crutches, trying to carry bags, slipping, falling, nearly crying, not from self-pity but from sheer frustration. The kind of frustration that boils up when your body won't do what your heart wants it to.

Weather adds another layer of complexity to life with mobility equipment. Rain makes surfaces slippery. Snow makes crutches sink. Ice makes everything treacherous. Cold makes metal equipment painful to touch. Heat makes leather straps uncomfortable against skin.

But the weather also taught me about preparation and contingency planning. I learned to check forecasts not just for comfort, but for safety. I learned to carry extra supplies in case equipment failed. I learned to have backup plans for getting from place to place when conditions made my usual methods impossible.

Teachers often told us to toughen up, to find strength we didn't think we had. Sometimes that worked, but more often it piled stress on top of exhaustion. I was forced to be creative, to solve problems, to figure out how to get from A to B in ways my peers never had to think about.

But the cost was high.

This "toughen up" mentality is one of the most problematic aspects of how society deals with disability. It suggests that our struggles are character-building rather than systemically imposed, that the solution to accessibility barriers is individual resilience rather than structural change.

While resilience is certainly valuable, it's important to recognize that this shouldn't be required. The goal should be to create systems that work for everyone, not to force some people to develop superhuman coping skills just to participate in basic activities.

People praised my strength, but strength shouldn't have been required just to get to class. The lesson of those winters wasn't toughness; it was clarity: that resilience is admirable, but accessibility is freedom.

The Isolation of Being Strong

There was no one to talk to, no safe space to admit how hard it was. Children with disabilities learn early not to complain, not to cry, not to appear weak, because we don't want to be labeled a burden.

This emotional isolation is one of the most damaging aspects of growing up with a disability. Just at the time when we're facing unique and significant challenges, we're also taught that expressing our feelings about those challenges is inappropriate, ungrateful, or weak.

The message is clear: if you're going to be different, at least be quietly different. If you're going to need accommodations, at least be cheerful about it. If you're going to struggle, at least struggle gracefully. Don't make others uncomfortable with your reality.

And then there was pity. If I disliked anything more than stares, it was pity. Sad eyes, tilted heads, voices softening as though I were fragile. I never wanted that. I didn't want sympathy; I wanted respect.

Pity is perhaps the most insidious form of discrimination because it masquerades as kindness. People who pity us often believe they're being compassionate, caring, generous. They don't realize that pity is fundamentally dehumanizing; that it positions us as objects of sympathy rather than subjects of our own lives.

Respect, on the other hand, recognizes our full humanity. Respect acknowledges that we face challenges without suggesting that those challenges define us. Respect offers support without condescension, assistance without assumption, kindness without patronization.

That was when I began to understand that real strength isn't about hiding pain, it's about defining the terms on which you're seen.

It took years before I could look back without bitterness, before I could see that the lessons I carried came intertwined with loss.

The Gifts Hidden in Struggle

What I didn't know then was that this daily negotiation with pain and visibility would later become my greatest preparation for leadership, the kind forged not in comfort, but in adaptation.

The truth is, there were no joyful memories with crutches. They made my shoulders ache, my hands blister, my body hurt in new ways. They limited my ability to dance, to run, to join games. They drew more attention when all I wanted was to belong.

And yet, they taught me things I couldn't have learned otherwise: creativity, problem-solving, and endurance.

This is the complex reality of adaptive equipment: it simultaneously limits and enables, restricts and empowers, isolates and connects. The device that makes some activities impossible makes other activities possible. The equipment that draws unwanted attention can also become a tool for advocacy and education.

Crutches taught me what it meant to keep moving even when it hurt, even when it felt unfair. This lesson in persistence would serve me well in every area of life in school, in work, in relationships, in advocacy. When you learn to keep going despite physical pain and social barriers, you develop a kind of mental toughness that can't be taught in any other way.

But it's important to be honest about the cost of this education. Yes, I learned valuable skills from using crutches. Yes, I developed resilience and creativity and problem-solving abilities. But I also experienced unnecessary pain, social isolation, and systemic barriers that could have been addressed through better design, better attitudes, and better support systems.

The goal isn't to glorify pain, but to recognize what it can teach us. Struggle isn't sacred, but it can be instructive. What looks like progress in motion can still feel like loss in belonging and both truths can exist at once.

CHAPTER 4

SUPPORTING A CHILD THROUGH TRANSITIONS

The transition to crutches often happens during adolescence, a time when young people are already navigating complex questions about identity, belonging, and independence. Adding the physical demands and social visibility of crutches to this developmental stage creates unique challenges that go far beyond simple mobility.

It's important to acknowledge that not every young person using crutches experiences the familiar landscape of school hallways, sports teams, and playground politics. I did not. My early education took place in special-education environments, where the social rhythms were very different and later, I avoided most physical activities altogether because the sense of vulnerability felt overwhelming.

There were no dramatic moments of being picked last for teams or classmates making a spectacle of me. Instead, the pain was quieter, more internal: the fear of being put into any situation where my limitations would be on display. The humiliation didn't come from peers, it came from the environment itself, from expectations I could never comfortably meet, and from the ache of always feeling like I was one misstep away from being exposed.

This chapter explores three interconnected dimensions of this transition: the physical realities of energy management, the emotional growth that comes from adaptation, and the systemic supports that make genuine inclusion possible. By understanding all three, adults can better help young people move from mere survival toward self-trust, resilience, and belonging.

Understanding the full impact of crutch use requires looking beyond biomechanics to examine energy systems, emotional labor, and social dynamics.

Energy Management: When Every Step Costs

For people who walk without assistive devices, movement is largely automatic. The body's energy expenditure during walking is so efficient that most people never consciously think about it. But for crutch users, every step requires conscious effort and significant energy.

Research on the metabolic cost of crutch use reveals striking findings: walking with crutches increases energy expenditure by 40-60% compared to other types of walking. For underarm crutches, which are most commonly prescribed to young people, the energy cost can be even higher, up to 77% greater than unassisted walking.

What does this mean in practical terms? A teenager using crutches to navigate a typical school day, walking between classes, climbing stairs, moving through crowded hallways, may expend as much energy as someone running several miles.

For many, the most humiliating moments weren't interpersonal; they were structural. Competitive activities, especially those involving speed, agility, or balance, placed their bodies in the spotlight in ways they never asked for. Even something as simple as a relay race or a group coordination exercise could feel like a public demonstration of everything they struggled with.

The dread of being assigned to activities that required children with disabilities to "keep up," knowing they couldn't. The embarrassment wasn't about losing; it was about being watched while losing. It was about the teacher waiting, the group waiting, everyone pretending the pacing was fine when it clearly wasn't. These moments weren't dramatic, but they left deep, lingering impressions about safety, worth, and belonging.

By the end of the day, they're not just tired; they're physiologically exhausted in ways that their peers cannot see or understand.

This invisible exhaustion creates what disability scholars call an "energy envelope," a finite amount of physical and cognitive energy available each day. People with limited energy envelopes must make constant calculations about how to allocate their resources: Which activities are essential? Which can be modified or eliminated? Where can energy be conserved for later needs?

But energy isn't just a medical measurement, it becomes a lived equation, shaping every decision a young person makes throughout their day.

Beneath the practical calculations lies another equation, one shaped by fear. The fear of being seen struggling can become its own form of exhaustion. Many young people, myself included, learned early to mask discomfort, to pre-plan routes that hid our limitations, and to avoid situations where the strain of movement would be visible.

Struggling in public carried a specific kind of vulnerability: the wobble that might draw attention, the stumble that could invite pity, the slow pace that felt like letting everyone down. This constant vigilance adds emotional weight to the already-heavy physical effort of moving through the world with crutches.

The Mathematics of Movement

For a crutch user, every activity becomes a complex equation:

Distance × terrain difficulty × load carried × time available = feasibility.

A task that seems simple, attending a class in a different building, requires calculating: How far? Are there stairs? Will I need to carry books? How much time between classes? Do I have enough energy left for the rest of the day?

This constant calculation develops sophisticated planning skills. Young people using crutches often become strategic thinkers earlier than their peers, out of necessity.

Strategic Adaptation

Energy management requires developing strategies that maximize function while minimizing cost:

Route optimization: Learning the most efficient paths through buildings, even if they're not the most direct.

Load reduction: Carrying only essential items, using wheeled backpacks, storing supplies in multiple locations.

Activity modification: Finding ways to participate in social activities that don't require extensive standing or walking.

Rest scheduling: Building in recovery time between high-energy activities.

Energy banking: Conserving energy on low-demand days to have reserves for high-demand occasions.

For some young people, especially those who grew up in special-education settings or who avoided physical environments altogether, strategy took a different form. Instead of learning how to participate, the strategy became learning how to *opt* out. Medical notes became shields, legitimate ones, but shields nonetheless, granting permission to avoid physical education classes, playground activities, or any space where physical performance was the expectation.

This wasn't laziness. It was self-protection. It was the quiet negotiation of dignity in environments that were never built with disabled bodies in mind. Many of us learned early that the safest option was to remove ourselves from the equation entirely.

For instance, one student I worked with learned to map her day like a marathon runner, plotting rest stops between classes, storing supplies in multiple classrooms, and keeping an extra set of shoes near her locker for rough weather days.

These adaptations require a level of self-awareness and planning that most adolescents haven't yet developed. In this sense, using crutches accelerates certain aspects of cognitive and emotional maturity.

Over time, these logistical strategies evolve into something deeper, each physical adaptation becomes a lesson in creativity, resilience, and problem-solving. What begins as a set of survival tactics eventually shapes how young people think, feel, and engage with the world around them. In this way, mastering crutch use becomes far more than a matter of mobility, it becomes training in adaptability itself.

What Crutches Teach Beyond Mobility

For young people using crutches, daily life becomes a masterclass in skills that most people don't develop until much later, if at all.

Innovation Under Constraint

When standard approaches don't work, crutch users must innovate, but not always in the context of team sports or typical school activities. For some of us, innovation meant figuring out how to navigate daily life discreetly: how to carry items without drawing attention, how to adapt classroom tasks, or how to reposition ourselves in a room so that standing or walking wouldn't be required.

Even something as simple as moving from one part of the classroom to another became a choreography of planning, balance, and strategic timing. Innovation wasn't about performing with others; it was about surviving environments that were never designed with our bodies in mind.

These daily innovations develop what psychologists call "practical intelligence"; the ability to adapt to, shape, and select environments to achieve your goals. This type of intelligence is often a better predictor of real-world success than traditional academic intelligence.

Emotional Regulation

Using crutches in public means managing others' reactions while managing your own emotions. You must navigate stares from strangers, intrusive questions about your condition, unwanted help from well-meaning people, barriers created by inaccessible design, social exclusion from activities, and frustration with your own limitations.

Learning to regulate emotions in the face of these challenges develops emotional intelligence; the ability to recognize, understand, and manage emotions in yourself and others. This skill becomes invaluable in leadership, relationship management, and professional success.

Systems Thinking

When you can't take accessibility for granted, you start seeing systems; how buildings are designed, how schools are organized, how social activities are structured. You notice which entrances have stairs and which have ramps, how furniture arrangement affects mobility, when activities are scheduled with insufficient transition time, and where policies create unnecessary barriers.

This awareness helps young people understand how systems interconnect and influence each other. People who think this way often become effective advocates for change because they can identify where small interventions create significant improvements.

Interdependence

American culture particularly valorizes independence; the ability to function without needing others. But using crutches teaches a more nuanced lesson: we are all interdependent, and needing help doesn't diminish your worth.

Crutch users must learn to ask for assistance when needed, accept help graciously, distinguish between helpful support and disempowering pity, and offer help to others despite or because of their own challenges.

This understanding of interdependence, forced by circumstances, often leads to stronger empathy and more authentic relationships.

Interdependence, when embraced rather than hidden, becomes the foundation of strong communities; it teaches us that well-being depends on shared care.

There is another form of interdependence that often goes unnamed: the relationship we develop with ourselves when we choose to withdraw. Self-exclusion is frequently misunderstood as avoidance, but for many disabled young people, it is a form of agency.

We learned to read environments instantly; identifying which activities would expose our limitations, which rooms lacked safe exits, which situations would demand more of us than we could give. Choosing not to participate was often an act of self-preservation, not self-defeat.

This internal negotiation; Should I try? Should I protect myself? is a developmental milestone rarely acknowledged. It reflects emotional intelligence, risk assessment, and deep self-awareness.

The Pity vs. Respect Spectrum

Whether in special-education environments or mainstream settings, one of the most emotionally taxing aspects of using crutches is managing how others interpret your body; teachers, strangers, medical professionals, parents, and sometimes peers.

The Pity Response

Characteristics: Sad expressions, tilted head, soft voice. Assumptions of tragedy and suffering. Offers of help that feel patronizing. Comments like "I'm so sorry" or "You're so brave."

Why it's harmful: Pity positions the crutch user as an object of sympathy rather than a subject with agency. It suggests that using crutches makes life not worth living fully, and it often comes with lowered expectations.

The Inspiration Response

Characteristics: "You're so inspiring!" or "I have no excuse to complain about my problems." Making the person feel like they exist to motivate others.

Why it's harmful: It objectifies people with disabilities, uses their existence for others' benefit, and suggests that ordinary activities are heroic simply because they're done with a disability.

The Curiosity Response

Characteristics: Invasive questions about diagnosis, prognosis, cause. Staring without acknowledgement. Treating the person as a medical case study.

Why it's problematic: While curiosity itself isn't necessarily bad, when it's expressed without regard for privacy or personhood, it reduces someone to their medical condition.

The Avoidance Response

Characteristics: Looking away determinedly. Avoiding interaction or conversation. Obvious discomfort. Talking to companions about the person rather than to them directly.

Why it's harmful: It treats disability as something shameful or uncomfortable, denies the person's humanity, and creates social isolation.

The Respect Response

Characteristics: Treating the person as a complete human being, not defined by equipment. Offering assistance by asking "Would you like help?" rather than assuming. Taking cues from the person about what they need. Engaging in natural social interaction. Acknowledging barriers are environmental, not individual.

Why it works: It recognizes that using crutches is one aspect of a person's life, not their entire identity, and it respects their agency and competence.

Respect doesn't always come naturally; it's modeled through example, and adults play a critical role in teaching it.

How to Respond to Problematic Reactions

Adults can help young people develop strategies for responding to problematic reactions:

For pity: "I appreciate your concern, but I'm doing well. My crutches help me get around effectively."

For inspiration comments: "I'm just living my life, like everyone else. Using crutches is just how I get around."

For invasive questions: "That's pretty personal. I'd rather talk about [change subject]" or "I prefer not to discuss my medical history."

For unsolicited help: "Thanks for offering, but I've got it. I'll let you know if I need help."

For avoidance: Directly engaging: "Hi, I'm [name]. How's your day going?" can break the ice and normalize interaction.

Teaching Others to Respond Appropriately

Adults can model respect by using appropriate language and attitudes:

For young children: "Everyone's body works differently. [Name]'s crutches help them walk, just like glasses help some people see."

For peers: Address disability matter-of-factly, focus on the person's interests and personality, and create opportunities for accessible participation.

For adults: Challenge assumptions, question why activities are structured in exclusionary ways, and advocate for universal design.

It's worth saying clearly what wasn't part of my story: I wasn't bullied by classmates, picked last for games, or publicly shamed by peers. My pain didn't come from cruelty; it came from misalignment. From being in environments that asked my body to perform in ways it simply couldn't.

The exclusion I felt was structural, not interpersonal. The humiliation was internal, not inflicted. And the protection I developed was adaptive, not antisocial.

These distinctions matter. They remind us that disability experiences are diverse, and that emotional wounds often come not from people, but from systems.

Creating Accessible Schools: Physical and Emotional

Creating truly accessible schools requires addressing both physical and emotional accessibility. True inclusion depends not just on ramps and elevators but on an environment that makes every student feel capable, respected, and part of the community.

Physical Accessibility Essentials Physical inclusion begins with infrastructure, ensuring that mobility never becomes a barrier to learning or belonging. Beyond legal requirements (ramps, elevators, accessible bathrooms), comprehensive physical accessibility includes:

- Adequate transition time between classes so students using crutches can move without rushing or risk of injury.
- Accessible seating near doors or adjustable furniture that doesn't isolate students from peers.
- Locker placement in convenient, low-traffic areas.
- Modified physical education expectations that build on students' abilities, not their limitations.
- Clear, practiced emergency plans that don't assume stair use or speed.
- Indoor routes and weather accommodations for safety during rain or snow.

Emotional Accessibility Essentials Equally vital is emotional access, cultivating belonging, dignity, and fairness in how students are treated and represented. Schools can foster emotional accessibility through:

- **Expectation fairness:** Holding students to the same academic standards while offering flexible methods for success.
- **Representation:** Including disability in literature, history, and cultural curriculum.
- **Language awareness:** Using terms that honor identity and preference, such as "disabled student" or "student who uses crutches."
- **Proactive accommodation:** Anticipating needs before they become barriers, offering notes, flexible timing, and adjusted classroom layouts.
- **Peer education:** Creating inclusive understanding through speakers, projects, and accessibility audits.
- **Anti-bullying strategies:** Training staff to spot subtle forms of exclusion and ensuring clear policies include disability-based bullying.
- **Social participation:** Designing activities and group work that value diverse contributions and make inclusion seamless, not exceptional.

Toolkit: What Adults Can Do Right Now

Knowledge becomes power when it's put into practice. The following tools translate the principles of energy management, emotional support, and inclusive design into daily actions that help children thrive through physical and social transitions.

What You Can Do Right Now:

- **Map the day together.** Sit down with the child to plan energy use. Identify moments that require more stamina and where rest can be built in.

- **Simplify logistics.** Advocate for early class dismissal or extra passing time to reduce hallway congestion and fatigue. Keep duplicate textbooks at home to lighten the load.
- **Adapt, don't exclude.** Modify activities so the child can still participate meaningfully, whether through strategy roles in sports or creative alternatives during physical games.
- **Normalize difference.** Talk openly with classmates or siblings about how everyone's body works differently and why accessibility matters to everyone.
- **Model calm confidence.** Your ease when interacting with the child in public teaches others how to engage with respect rather than pity.
- **Ask before helping.** "Would you like help carrying that?" honors agency more than assuming assistance is needed.
- **Offer small choices.** Let the child decide how and when to use supports when possible. This builds ownership and self-advocacy.
- **Connect to role models.** Introduce stories or mentors who use similar equipment, showing that independence and success coexist with support.
- **Advocate systemically.** Push for accessible design in schools, sports, and community spaces. Help others see that accessibility isn't charity, it's equity.

Daily Habits That Help:

True inclusion lives in the everyday moments. Here are a few small habits that build long-term confidence and trust:

- **Check in, don't check out.** Ask daily, "How's your energy today?" to help children learn to read their own limits.
- **Celebrate micro-wins.** Notice effort, not endurance: "You managed those stairs today even though you were tired. That's self-awareness."

- **Adjust expectations together.** If fatigue sets in, pivot without guilt. Teach that adaptability is strength, not failure.
- **Prioritize rest as skill-building.** Schedule rest like homework; recovery is part of growth, not an interruption of it.
- **End the day with gratitude.** Encourage reflection on one thing that felt easier or better today. It reinforces progress, not perfection.

What to Watch For:

Adjustment takes time. Persistent patterns can signal that a child needs additional support. Use these signs as cues for conversation, not correction:

- **Withdrawal or social isolation.** May indicate the child feels "othered" or invisible. Invite participation in low-pressure settings.
- **Silence about challenges.** Can mean they've learned their struggles aren't welcome. Create safe spaces for honesty without penalty.
- **Self-blame or "burden" talk.** Signals shame. Reframe by emphasizing how everyone needs accommodations in different ways.
- **Physical symptoms of overexertion.** Persistent pain or skin irritation calls for medical reassessment and emotional reassurance.
- **Mood changes.** Irritability, sadness, or anxiety often reflect fatigue or social stress rather than personality shifts.
- **Overachievement or perfectionism.** May suggest they feel pressure to "prove" themselves. Model rest as responsible, not lazy.

If these signs appear, invite an open conversation without judgment. Sometimes what a child needs most is permission to admit that things are hard without fear of losing autonomy or opportunity.

How to Keep Perspective:

Progress isn't linear. Some days will feel seamless; others will feel heavy. What matters most is consistency, not flawlessness.

When adults model flexibility and grace, children learn that their worth isn't tied to productivity or physical performance. Every setback can become a lesson in resilience, not because it's easy, but because it's shared.

Remember: you don't have to have all the answers. You just have to show up, listen, and adapt together.

Key Takeaway:

Independence doesn't mean isolation. It means having the right support in place to live fully. True strength comes from interdependence: knowing when to rely on systems, when to self-advocate, and when to extend that same understanding to others.

PART III

The Young Adult's View
Reclaiming Visibility

CHAPTER 5

WALKING WITH A CANE

Finding Power in Visibility

The Professional Stage

The elevator doors slid open, and I stepped into the marble lobby, cane in hand. My heels clicked against the floor, but it wasn't the shoes that caught attention; it was the cane. Eyes followed me as I walked toward the conference room, every stare heavy with unspoken questions.

This moment represents a crucial transition in any disability journey: the move from childhood, where you're primarily someone's child who happens to have a disability, to adulthood, where you become a professional who happens to use adaptive equipment.

This chapter explores how visibility, once a source of discomfort, can evolve into a form of power, creativity, and connection.

In childhood, your disability is often managed by others; parents, teachers, medical professionals. You're the recipient of care, the object of interventions, the beneficiary of accommodations. In adulthood, you become responsible for managing your own disability, advocating for your own needs, and navigating systems that weren't designed with you in mind.

Inside, my colleagues were already seated around the long conference table. This was my meeting to call to order. As I entered, I could feel my pulse quicken. I straightened my shoulders, adjusted my jacket, and forced a calm smile, willing myself to appear seamless, graceful, and professional.

But balancing a cane, a briefcase, and the expectations of leadership was anything but seamless.

Campus buildings had steps with no ramps. Classrooms were on upper floors with no elevators. Bathrooms were too narrow for wheelchairs. Every single day was a battle just to access the education I was paying for.

But I refused to be shut out. If a building wasn't accessible, I made noise until it was. If a professor didn't understand, I educated them. I had to advocate for myself constantly, because no one else was going to do it.

Employers saw the wheelchair before they saw my qualifications. I had to work twice as hard to prove I could do the job, then work again to make the physical space accessible so I could actually do it.

Simple things other employees took for granted - getting to the bathroom, accessing the break room, reaching file cabinets - became negotiations and modifications I had to request and often fight for.

Reaching the head of the table, I placed my notes down and leaned the cane discreetly at my side. In that instant, I wasn't just a young woman leading a professional team. I was different. Not sick, not broken, yet to others, that's what the cane suggested.

This is the challenge of visible disability in professional settings: before you even open your mouth, people have made assumptions about your capabilities, your limitations, your role in the organization. Your equipment becomes a louder statement than your qualifications, your experience, or your ideas.

The Internal Storm

What no one could see was the private storm inside me. The tears shed the night before. The embarrassment of carrying a device I had always associated with age, frailty, or sickness. The frustration of knowing that before I even spoke a word, I already stood apart not for my voice, my authority, or my ideas, but for the cane in my hand.

This internal conflict is something that many people with visible disabilities experience but rarely discuss. There's a difference between accepting your disability intellectually and being comfortable with its visibility emotionally. You can understand that your equipment is just a tool while still feeling self-conscious about using it in public. You can advocate for disability rights while still sometimes wishing you could be invisible.

These feelings aren't a failure of self-acceptance, nor do they require labeling other people. They arise because our world often responds to visible differences with discomfort, confusion, or misplaced concern. Those reactions are shaped by culture, not by malice, and they accumulate quietly inside the person who is being perceived.

When I first began using a cane in my twenties, the experience was devastating. I was young, stepping into my professional career, attending important meetings, representing my boss at social events, traveling, and networking with dignitaries. And here I was, forced to explain what this cane meant.

People always asked, "What happened? What's wrong with you?" They assumed illness. They assumed frailty. Rarely did they see me as a young woman simply living her life, using the tool she needed to do her job.

What people also didn't see was the loneliness that came with these moments. Visibility is paradoxical. You are constantly being noticed, but not truly seen. The gaze lingers, but it never lands on your humanity. There is a strange isolation in walking into a room and feeling every pair of eyes track the cane first and your face second. It creates a split within you: the person you know yourself to be, and the version reflected back by strangers who have already formed stories about you. That gap can feel cavernous.

This constant need to explain, justify, and educate becomes exhausting. It means that every interaction contains an element of disability advocacy, whether you want it to or not. It means that you're never just a colleague, just a friend, just a person going about their business. You're always also a representative of the disability community, a teaching opportunity, an inspiration or a tragedy depending on how the observer chooses to frame your existence.

Adolescence and early adulthood bring new layers of visibility. For young people, a cane can shift how others see them before they even speak. Parents who've watched their children navigate braces and crutches may feel relief that their child has "graduated" to something more manageable, but for the young person, a cane in professional or social settings carries its own weight of judgment and assumption.

The body always carries the echoes of our emotions. And then there is the vigilance, the ceiling-level awareness that never turns off. Every doorway becomes a calculation. Every floor surface a risk assessment. Every social interaction a negotiation between wanting to appear effortless and knowing that effort is always required. People see the cane; they do not see the mental checklist behind every step: *Where should I stand? Will someone bump me? Is there a chair nearby? What if I drop something? What if I fall?*

This constant scanning is its own form of fatigue, quiet, consuming, invisible.

The shame, tension, and vigilance I felt inside showed up in my posture, my gait, and the ache that spread across my shoulders.

The Physical Reality

Physically, the cane was exhausting. It strained my wrist and hips. It meant leaning into pain to remain standing, smiling through the discomfort while balancing a wine glass in one hand and the cane in the other.

This is another hidden reality of adaptive equipment: it doesn't eliminate pain or effort. It just redistributes it. The cane took weight off my legs but put strain on my arms and shoulders. It helped me balance but created new pressure points. It enabled me to walk longer distances but required constant conscious attention to how I was positioning my body.

Research shows that walking with a cane can increase total energy expenditure by 20 to 30 percent, depending on gait and terrain, proof that what looks effortless often isn't.

More than once, someone would bump into it, causing me to stumble. I remember walking across a busy Chicago street one morning, only to hear a truck driver yell out his window, "You should be home taking care of that!" He had seen the cane and assumed sickness, weakness, incapacity.

This public commentary on our bodies and our choices is something that people with visible disabilities learn to expect. Strangers feel entitled to offer opinions about our equipment, our appearance, our presence in public spaces. They make assumptions about what we should or shouldn't be doing, where we should or shouldn't be going, how we should be spending our time.

Walking into public spaces becomes an emotional tightrope. You brace yourself for the stares that linger too long, the whispered conversations that end abruptly when you approach, the well-meaning strangers who swoop in with questions or unsolicited advice. None of this is catastrophic on its own, but accumulated over years, it creates a weight you carry inside your chest. A heaviness that says, "You are being watched. You are being assessed. Be careful."

It's a burden people rarely acknowledge because the world equates youth with invisibility and ease. But for those of us with visible differences, every outing can feel like stepping onto a stage we never auditioned for.

The assumption that using a cane means you should be "home taking care of that" reveals deep-seated beliefs about disability and productivity. It suggests that people with disabilities are not expected to be contributing members of society, that our role is to be cared for rather than to care for others, that our proper place is private rather than public.

These reactions aren't about "bad people." They are about inherited assumptions and old ideas absorbed without question. Most individuals never reflect on why a cane signals illness, fragility, or limitation to them; the story was written long before they encountered us. Naming these patterns isn't about accusation. It's about understanding the landscape we navigate every day.

The Art of Reclamation

But even as people stared, judged, or pitied, the cane became something I could reclaim. I began to search for canes that fit my style, my personality. At first, it was impossible. They were all orthopedic, medical, and ugly. Then I started embellishing them myself, covering them with fabric, adding stones, creating handles that felt elegant.

What I didn't expect was how emotional that transformation would be. Holding a cane that finally felt like *mine* softened something inside me, an internal resistance I had carried for years. For the first time, I wasn't just compensating for a weakness. I was choosing beauty in a place where the world expected sorrow. That choice was an act of quiet rebellion.

This process of customization was about more than aesthetics. It was about refusing to accept that adaptive equipment had to look medical, institutional, or apologetic. It was about claiming the right to express my personality through my tools, just as others might express themselves through their clothing, jewelry, or accessories.

Friends began to bring me canes from their travels, one from the Philippines, another from Mexico, another from Africa, and even a beautiful one from China. Each cane became a fashion statement, a story, an expression of who I was rather than what I lacked.

This transformation of my cane from medical device to fashion accessory was also a transformation of my relationship with my disability. Instead of trying to hide or minimize my difference, I was celebrating it. Instead of apologizing for my equipment, I was making it beautiful. Instead of seeing my cane as a symbol of limitation, I was making it a symbol of creativity and self-expression.

This process of reclamation taking something that society sees as negative and finding ways to make it positive is a crucial part of developing a healthy relationship with disability. It doesn't mean denying the real challenges or pretending everything is easy. It means refusing to accept other people's definitions of what your life should look like.

In transforming my cane, I joined a quiet revolution, one where design becomes declaration, and disability becomes a site of innovation rather than apology.

The Unexpected Door

Eventually, my professional path reached a crossroads. My administrative government job had become unsustainable. My disability and the lack of accommodations made it impossible to continue.

The silence of that last office day was heavy: the hum of fluorescent lights, the slow packing of files, the sound of my cane tapping one last time on the marble floor. But that silence became space for something new. Leaving it was a painful decision, but it opened the door to something unexpected.

I began designing footwear for people with hard-to-fit feet, something I never imagined I would do.

This career transition illustrates an important principle: sometimes what looks like failure or limitation is actually redirection toward your true calling. The barriers I faced in traditional employment forced me to consider alternatives I never would have explored otherwise.

Shoes had never been a source of joy for me; I couldn't buy them off the rack. But designing them? That changed everything.

For most people, shopping for shoes is a pleasure: an expression of personal style, a small luxury, a form of self-care. For people with disabilities, shopping for shoes is often an exercise in frustration. Feet that are different sizes, braces that require extra room, circulation issues that demand specific materials, mobility concerns that prioritize function over fashion. These realities are rarely addressed by mainstream footwear designers.

But what if they were? What if shoes could be both functional and beautiful? What if adaptive design could be an elegant design? What if the market for "special needs" footwear could be transformed into a market for innovative, inclusive fashion?

The Birth of an Entrepreneur

This was the beginning of my transformation. The cane allowed me to lean into fashion and creativity. I began coordinating it with my shoes, my hats, my entire look. People stopped me on the street to ask where I had found my shoes, and I could proudly say, "I designed and made them."

For the first time, I was not just a professional hiding behind pain: I was a designer, an artist, a woman creating beauty out of necessity.

This shift from hiding to showcasing, from apologizing to celebrating, represents a fundamental change in how I understood my relationship with disability. Instead of seeing my adaptive needs as problems to be solved, I began seeing them as design challenges to be embraced. Instead of trying to fit into a world that wasn't made for me, I began creating a world that could include me.

The cane didn't erase the exhaustion or the strain. But it opened doors, literal and creative. It made me visible again. People saw me, and I began to see myself differently too.

That visibility gave me courage to build something new. The studio, the sketches, the first prototypes, they were all experiments in freedom. I wasn't chasing perfection anymore; I was learning to design from imperfection, to honor the beauty of what already was.

Each creation told part of my story: bold colors, uneven lines, circles that never quite closed but still held everything together. What began as a tool for mobility became a language of design, a way to reclaim both space and self.

This is the paradox of visible disability: the very thing that makes life more difficult in some ways can also make life more meaningful. The visibility that draws unwanted attention can also create opportunities for connection, education, and advocacy. The equipment that marks you as different can also become a tool for building community and inspiring innovation.

Love in the Time of Visibility

Socially, the cane also carried weight. As a young woman, I worried about dating, about being seen as desirable. One of my deepest fears, the one I could barely admit to myself: Who would want someone with a cane? Would I ever be a prospect for love, for marriage, for family?

Society had already told me in a thousand ways that women with disabilities weren't seen as sexual beings. We weren't supposed to be desired, to date, to have romantic relationships. The message was clear: your body is now medical, not sensual. You're a patient, not a woman.

I grieved the loss of being seen. Not just as capable or independent but as desirable. As someone who could be wanted.

These concerns about romantic relationships are among the most painful aspects of living with visible disability, but they're rarely discussed openly. We're supposed to be focused on higher things, inspiration, overcoming, achievement, not on the very human desire for love, partnership, and physical intimacy.

But of course, we have these desires. Of course, we worry about whether potential partners will see past our equipment to the person underneath. Of course, we wonder whether our disabilities will be deal-breakers in relationships, whether we'll be seen as burdens rather than partners, whether we'll be loved in spite of our differences rather than because of our wholeness.

People even asked invasive questions: "Can you have children? Will you ever be able to?" At times, I felt more like a defective machine than a human being. Those were painful years of doubt and loneliness.

The loneliness didn't always come from being alone. It came from the fear that no one would ever understand the full weight I carried. The stares on the street, the questions in professional settings, the constant body awareness, it all created a kind of emotional distance even in the presence of others. I sometimes wondered whether anyone could meet me in that space without flinching or pulling away.

But visibility, once my deepest fear, became the very thing that made me recognizable to someone who could truly see me.

Love Sees Everything

And yet, life surprised me. Over time, people began to see me not for the cane but for my courage, my creativity, my spirit. A man once read about me and my designs in a newspaper article, the same article that mentioned the cane I used, and years later, he sought me out. He saw not a woman defined by disability, but a woman of strength, elegance, and artistry.

He pursued me, and eventually, he became my husband, the man I had always hoped for.

This story matters because it challenges the narrative that people with disabilities must settle for less in relationships, that we should be grateful for anyone who will have us, that our disabilities necessarily limit our romantic prospects.

The truth is more complex and more hopeful. Yes, some people will be deterred by visible disability. Yes, dating can be more complicated when you use adaptive equipment. Yes, there are additional conversations to be had, additional considerations to be navigated.

But there are also people who see disability as part of the full human experience rather than as a detraction from it. There are people who are attracted to strength, resilience, and creativity rather than put off by the tools that enable those qualities. There are people who understand that love is about seeing and accepting the whole person, strengths and challenges, abilities and limitations, equipment and all.

The cane, which I once believed marked the end of my dreams, had in fact opened the path to one of the greatest joys of my life.

The Bridge to Possibility

Looking back, I see now that the cane was never a symbol of weakness; it was a bridge. It carried me from one version of myself to another. It forced me to confront shame, judgment, and pain, but it also gave me the chance to embrace creativity, reinvention, and love.

It was never just a stick to lean on. It was a companion in my journey, a reminder that we are more than the tools we carry, more than the labels society gives us.

But even that companionship carried weight. Some days the cane felt like an ally; other days it felt like a spotlight. I learned that healing wasn't just physical, it was emotional. It required acknowledging the grief of visibility, the exhaustion of always adjusting, the sorrow of being misunderstood, and the bravery of stepping out in public anyway.

Visibility may empower us, but it also exposes us. And living between those two truths is its own lifelong practice.

This shift, seeing equipment as companion rather than burden, does not require categorizing or blaming others. It simply means choosing the narrative that supports our well-being. The world may still default to old assumptions, but we do not have to carry those assumptions inside us. We can create our own meaning, grounded in dignity, truth, and lived experience.

I never liked the word "special" when applied to children or adults with disabilities. Special becomes a label, a reminder of difference, an excuse for pity. I didn't want to be "special." I wanted to be seen as myself.

The language we use to describe disability matters enormously. "Special" sounds positive but actually creates distance; it suggests that people with disabilities exist in a separate category from "normal" people, that we need different treatment, that we're fundamentally other.

The cane was not a badge of illness, not a mark of weakness. It was no different than a pair of glasses, a computer, or a pen, just another tool that allowed me to function, create, and live.

This normalization of adaptive equipment is crucial for changing social attitudes. When we present our tools as ordinary rather than tragic, as functional rather than medical, as chosen rather than imposed, we help others understand that disability is simply another way of being human.

What mattered was how I chose to use it. I could let it define me, or I could let it free me. I chose freedom.

This choice to frame our equipment as freeing rather than limiting is available to anyone who uses adaptive tools. It's not about denying the real challenges or pretending everything is easy. It's about recognizing that we have agency in how we understand our own experience, how we present ourselves to the world, and how we define what's possible for our lives.

The cane became a fashion statement and a declaration of identity. The cane became my teacher, reminding me that visibility isn't a threat to overcome but a truth to embody, a way to stand taller in a world that still learns how to see.

CHAPTER 6

HELPING YOUNG ADULTS RECLAIM CONFIDENCE

The cane occupies a unique position in the hierarchy of mobility devices. Unlike braces, which can be hidden under clothing, or wheelchairs, which are obviously disability-related, the cane exists in a liminal space. It's visible but often ambiguous. It announces differences without always explaining it. And crucially, it can become a canvas for self-expression in ways that other mobility devices rarely allow.

This chapter explores how adults can help young people move from seeing visibility as exposure to embracing it as empowerment, reframing the cane not as a mark of limitation but as a tool for identity, confidence, and connection.

Understanding how to support young adults using canes requires examining how visibility shapes identity, how stigma can be transformed, and how design choices become declarations of autonomy.

Visibility as Power, Not Shame

Traditional disability narratives have framed visibility as a problem to be solved. The goal, whether stated explicitly or not, has been to minimize the appearance of difference, to "pass" as non-disabled whenever possible, to make adaptive equipment as inconspicuous as can be managed.

But this approach fundamentally misunderstands the relationship between visibility and power. Recent disability scholarship has challenged the assumption that invisibility is always preferable. When young people stop trying to hide their differences and instead claim them as part of their identity, they shift from shame to pride, from apology to assertion.

For many young adults, this empowerment begins as tension, a tug-of-war between the desire to be seen and the fear of being misread. Visibility is powerful, but it also exposes. The challenge isn't erasing that discomfort, but learning to live through it with dignity.

The Visibility Paradox

For young adults using canes, visibility creates a paradox:

Professional contexts: Visibility can trigger assumptions about incapability, leading to discrimination in hiring, promotion, and task assignment.

Social contexts: Visibility can lead to unwanted attention, invasive questions, and objectification.

Personal contexts: Visibility requires deciding whether the cane defines you or is simply one aspect of who you are.

But visibility also offers advantages:

Authenticity: No energy wasted on concealment or pretense.

Community: Visible disability can facilitate connections with other disabled people.

Advocacy: Visibility makes you a representative, which can be exhausting but also empowering.

Education: Your presence challenges assumptions and expands others' understanding.

The key is helping young adults develop what psychologists call "disability pride", a positive relationship with disability identity that neither minimizes real challenges nor accepts societal devaluation.

Stages of Accepting Visibility

Young people often move through stages in their relationship with visibility. Understanding these stages can help adults support them more effectively:

Stage 1: Denial/Minimization "My cane doesn't mean I'm disabled" or "It's just temporary" Focus: Distancing from disability identity.

Stage 2: Awareness/Resistance "I hate that people stare" or "I wish I didn't need this" Focus: Recognizing difference but resenting it.

Stage 3: Exploration/Questioning "What does using a cane mean for my identity?" or "Who else uses canes?" Focus: Investigating disability culture and community.

Stage 4: Integration/Pride "My cane is part of who I am" or "I'm proud to be disabled" Focus: Incorporating disability into holistic self-concept.

Stage 5: Advocacy/Leadership "I use my visibility to create change" or "My experience gives me unique insights" Focus: Leveraging disability experience for social impact.

Not everyone moves through these stages linearly, and movement can be triggered by life transitions, community connections, or cultural exposure. Adults can help by recognizing where a young person is and creating opportunities for growth without forcing it.

One college student I spoke with described starting in denial, hiding her cane in photos, before slowly decorating it with floral tape and eventually leading her school's accessibility task force. The cane didn't change, but her story about it did.

Self-Expression Through Design

One of the most powerful ways that cane users transform visibility from burden to asset is through design personalization. When a cane becomes an expression of personality rather than a mark of medicalization, it fundamentally shifts the meaning of the device.

Why Design Matters

Fashion and accessories serve multiple functions beyond utility. What we choose to put on our bodies tells a story about who we are and who we want to be.

For people using mobility devices, the historical message has been: your equipment is medical, not personal. It should be neutral, clinical, apologetic. Chrome and beige. Institutional and forgettable.

But this approach denies disabled people the same opportunity for self-expression that others take for granted. When someone chooses red shoes or a patterned tie, they're expressing personality. Why should a cane be different?

The Power of Reclamation

When cane users begin customizing their devices, adding color, pattern, embellishments, or choosing non-traditional materials, they're taking an object that society codes as shameful and redefining it as beautiful, interesting, or powerful.

This process has psychological benefits:

Agency and Control: Choosing how the cane looks returns control over presentation. Instead of accepting what the medical system provides, the young person becomes the designer of their own image.

Narrative Reframing: A decorated cane tells a different story than a medical one. It says: "This is a fashion choice, not a medical tragedy."

Conversation Starter: When people comment on a beautiful cane, the conversation shifts from "What's wrong with you?" to "Where did you get that?" This reframes the interaction from pity to admiration.

Community Building: Distinctive canes can signal membership in the disability community and attract connections with others who understand reclamation.

Joy and Playfulness: Choosing fun designs reminds us that disability doesn't preclude beauty, pleasure, or aesthetics.

When young people reclaim their equipment as art, they don't just reshape their self-image, they participate in redesigning what society imagines disability can look like.

Supporting Self-Expression

Adults can support young people's design choices by:

- Treating cane customization as understandable self-expression, not frivolity.
- Helping them find or create personalized designs.
- Celebrating their choices without making them feel like they're performing inspiration.
- Connecting them with disabled designers and artists.
- Never suggesting they should make their equipment "less noticeable".

The Role of Representation

The stories a culture tells about disability shape how disabled people see themselves and how they're treated by others. For most of media history, disability representation has been limited to a few recurring tropes: the villain, the inspirational saint, or the pitied victim.

How many times have we seen a disabled character who exists only to teach a lesson to someone else? These portrayals don't just shape how society sees disability; they teach young disabled people how to see themselves.

Problematic Patterns

Common patterns in disability representation include:

The Super Cripple: A disabled person with extraordinary abilities that "compensate" for disability. Problem: Suggests disability is only acceptable if offset by exceptional abilities.

The Charity Case: A disabled person whose role is to receive help and inspire pity. Problem: Denies disabled people agency and complex motivation.

The Bitter Cripple: A disabled person whose bitterness makes them antagonistic. Problem: Conflates disability with moral failure.

The Magical Cure: A story that ends with disability being eliminated. Problem: Implies disabled life isn't worth living.

The Inspirational Object: A disabled person who exists to inspire non-disabled characters. Problem: Objectifies disabled people.

Better Representation

Effective disability representation should:

- Feature disabled actors playing disabled characters.

- Show disability as one aspect of a complex character, not their only trait.
- Depict realistic accommodations without making them dramatic plot points.
- Include disability across genres (not just medical dramas).
- Show disabled people in romantic relationships, as parents, in professional roles.
- Portray both challenges and joys of disabled life.

Research consistently shows that media representation affects real-world attitudes and behaviors. When young people see authentic disability representation, it shapes how they understand themselves and their possibilities.

How Adults Can Help

You can support positive representation by:

- Watching shows and reading books featuring disabled characters together.
- Discussing how disability is portrayed in the media.
- Following disabled creators on social media.
- Encouraging young people to create their own representations.
- Challenging stereotypes when you encounter them.

Universal Design and Cultural Change

Universal design doesn't just remove barriers; it reimagines what inclusion means. That way, no one feels like an afterthought. Ramps, captions, and automatic doors aren't special features; they're reminders that the world works better when it's built for everyone.

Examples All Around Us

Many features now considered standard were initially designed for disability access:

Curb cuts: Designed for wheelchair users, now used by parents with strollers, delivery workers, cyclists, and travelers with luggage.

Automatic doors: Designed for mobility disabilities, now used by people carrying packages and anyone preferring convenience.

Text-to-speech: Designed for blind users, now used for audiobooks, navigation, and hands-free device operation.

Closed captioning: Designed for deaf users, now used in noisy environments, language learning, and content in non-native languages.

This pattern reveals an important truth: designing for disability often creates innovations that benefit everyone. When we expand our definition of who we're designing for, we create better solutions.

Cultural Shifts Through Design

Universal design doesn't just make physical spaces more accessible; it changes how we think about bodies, ability, and belonging.

When environments are designed for diverse users from the start, disability becomes unremarkable. Children growing up in universally designed schools absorb the message that bodies come in many forms and all deserve accommodation.

When accessible design is beautiful, it challenges the association between disability and ugliness. When disabled people are visible using stylish equipment, it normalizes disability in public consciousness.

Just as architecture can embody inclusion, so too can personal design choices. The cane becomes a microcosm of the same principle; every detail communicates belonging.

The Cane as Declaration

The transformation of a cane from shameful necessity to proud declaration is about more than personal acceptance. It's about cultural reclamation.

When young people hide their canes, they reinforce the message that disability should be invisible, that difference is shameful, that medical equipment is apologetic by nature.

When they use their canes visibly and without apology, they challenge those assumptions. When they make them beautiful, they insist that disabled people deserve beauty. When they talk about them openly, they normalize disability.

The young professional who coordinates her cane with her outfit isn't being frivolous; she's engaging in resistance. She's refusing the mandate to minimize her difference. She's claiming the same right to self-expression that non-disabled people take for granted.

Toolkit: What Adults Can Do Right Now

Understanding the psychology of visibility is only the first step; true empowerment happens through daily practice. These tools help adults translate awareness into action, supporting young adults in reclaiming confidence, creativity, and control of their story.

What You Can Do Right Now:

Normalize visibility. Talk about the cane as naturally as you would about a backpack or pair of glasses. Normalize its presence by removing pity or tension from your tone.

Support personalization. Encourage young adults to decorate, paint, or accessorize their cane as a form of self-expression. Treat it as an extension of identity, not a medical device.

Model confidence. When you encounter stares or awkward moments, respond with calm ease. Your comfort helps shape how others, including the young person, interpret visibility.

Invite conversation. Ask, "How do you want to talk about your cane?" or "What do you want others to know?" This empowers self-advocacy and helps them shape their own narrative.

Encourage social participation. Help them navigate events, clubs, or activities without avoidance. Visibility should never mean withdrawal; it should mean entry on their own terms.

Amplify representation. Share stories, art, or social media accounts of creators and professionals who use canes or mobility aids proudly. Representation rewires what's possible.

Address language gently. Model inclusive phrasing, say "uses a cane" instead of "confined to a cane." Small language shifts change how people are perceived and how they perceive themselves.

Daily Habits That Help:

Confidence grows in moments of repetition and small choices. These daily habits help young adults build self-assurance through visibility rather than despite it:

- **Start with self-check-ins.** Ask, "How do you feel about using your cane today?" Listening first teaches that emotional responses are valid, not shameful.
- **Notice micro-wins.** Celebrate small victories like using the cane in a crowded space or taking a new route. Confidence builds in increments.

- **Use positive reflection.** Replace "You did so well" with "You looked so confident navigating that room." Reinforce identity, not performance.
- **Encourage self-pacing.** Some days will be easier than others. Teach that slowing down or taking breaks isn't weakness; it's wisdom.
- **End the day with affirmation.** A quiet reminder "Your strength isn't in hiding; it's in being seen" helps internalize pride rather than apology.

What to Watch For:

Confidence building isn't linear. These signs may indicate that a young person needs extra support, reflection, or reassurance.

- **Avoidance or concealment.** Hiding or downplaying the cane may signal internalized stigma. Respond by normalizing and celebrating its visibility.
- **Frustration or anger about stares.** Encourage open conversation; acknowledge that public gaze can hurt, and validate their feelings before offering advice.
- **Withdrawal from social spaces.** Help them identify accessible environments where they can participate comfortably and rebuild trust.
- **Self-deprecating humor.** While laughter can deflect tension, consistent self-mockery may hide deeper shame. Counter gently with affirming language.
- **Perfectionism or burnout.** Overcompensating to "prove" ability often leads to exhaustion. Reinforce that resting or asking for help shows maturity, not weakness.

If these patterns persist, focus on empathy and agency. Ask open-ended questions, listen more than you speak, and remind them that identity is built through honesty, not hiding.

How to Keep Perspective:

Confidence isn't built by doing everything right; it's built by showing up with consistency and compassion. Some days visibility will feel heavy; others, it will feel natural. What matters is helping young people see that confidence doesn't mean the absence of doubt; it means courage in its presence.

You don't have to fix every discomfort. Sometimes, the most healing thing you can do is to stand beside them, steady and unafraid of being seen together.

Key Takeaway:

A cane isn't a symbol of frailty; it's a declaration of autonomy. When young adults understand that visibility can be power, they stop apologizing for differences and start defining what confidence looks like on their own terms.

PART IV
The Wheelchair as Freedom

CHAPTER 7

FREEDOM IN MOTION

Before I ever rolled forward in a wheelchair, there was another vehicle that taught me what freedom felt like; my red Toyota Celica. And not long after, a red wheelchair to match. Those two flashes of color, car and chair, became symbols of fire and movement in a world that kept trying to slow me down.

When I first bought that Celica, I felt something ignite inside me. The moment I slid behind the wheel, wrapped my fingers around the leather, and heard the engine kick awake, I felt possibility crackling through me. I wasn't just driving; I was flying. The wind against my face, the roar of the road beneath me, the sun catching the red paint like a flame. I felt unstoppable.

I used to place my wheelchair in the back seat and drive on the highway, feeling so free with my hair blowing in the wind. It felt like the movies always depicted it.

I didn't fully understand it then, but the Celica was my first taste of what it meant to move *my way* without apology, without permission, without performing strength or pretending ease. The car didn't question my body. It didn't calculate my steps, or judge my pace, or require explanations. It simply carried me.

Years later, when I finally accepted the red wheelchair, that same feeling came rushing back but this time it lived inside me, not under the hood of a car.

The Red Convertible

The wheelchair sat in my living room for three months before I used it consistently.

It wasn't that I didn't need it; my body had been making that clear for years. Every trip to the grocery store left me exhausted for days. Walking through airports meant arriving at my destination already depleted. Professional events that should have energized me instead drained every reserve I had.

But needing something and accepting it are entirely different matters.

The chair was red. I'd insisted on that. If I was going to use a wheelchair, it wouldn't be institutional gray or apologetic beige. It would be bold, unapologetic, mine.

It matched the spirit of my old red Celica, the first machine that ever made me feel powerful. That car had given me a sense of speed I could never achieve on foot, a feeling of fire in my chest as the world blurred around me. The wheelchair carried a quieter fire, but a fire nonetheless.

In a strange way, the chair felt like an evolution of that freedom. Not in horsepower, but in selfhood. The Celica had let me outrun my limits; the wheelchair, I would later learn, would let me *embrace* them without losing momentum.

The sales representative seemed encouraged by my color choice as rarely someone would choose red, especially a professional woman.

The chair was a reminder of what I needed to learn and overcome. No one had really taught me how to use it. I had no Physical Therapist or

Occupational Therapist or Psychologist that would help me deal with all the emotions or how to go over cracks, or to avoid pebbles, stones or wooden sticks. How to manage the snow, ice or any sort of obstacle.

I was nervous, scared.

Fear of going outdoors and not knowing what to do.

Feeling trapped by what I imagined, of being easy prey for robbers and violators.

The pressure to be standing, walking, looking "normal" was everywhere. This was a time when the world felt like it was closing in on people with disabilities. Doors weren't wide enough. Nothing was automated. Public transportation was a nightmare, completely inaccessible.

I wasn't just afraid of using a wheelchair. I was afraid of becoming invisible, of being shut out from the world entirely. Because that's what happened to people like me back then. We disappeared.

The Weight of Symbols

A wheelchair meant something in my mind, something I'd spent my entire life trying not to be. It meant giving up. It meant admitting defeat. It meant that all the surgeries, all the pain, all the years of pushing through exhaustion had led to this: confinement.

That word "confined." I'd heard it so many times. "Confined to a wheelchair." "Wheelchair-bound." As though the chair were a prison rather than a possibility. I thought the chair would take something from me. I didn't yet understand that it would give me back everything I'd been losing.

I'd built my identity on walking. Yes, with braces, then crutches, then canes, but walking nonetheless. I was the woman who climbed stairs when elevators were broken. The professional who navigated conferences despite the physical cost. The designer who stood at her workbench for hours, even when her body screamed for rest.

Walking meant independence. Walking meant capability. Walking meant I wasn't really disabled, not disabled enough to need a wheelchair, anyway.

This is the lie I'd been telling myself: that some disabilities are acceptable while others are shameful, that mobility devices exist in a hierarchy, that a cane is dignified but a wheelchair is defeat.

The Breaking Point

The decision came not through epiphany but through exhaustion.

I had been invited to speak at a conference, a significant opportunity, the kind that could open doors professionally. The venue was large and spread across multiple buildings. My presentation was strong. My message mattered. But by the afternoon session, I could barely stand.

I sat alone at a corner, meditating on the silence. A colleague asked how I was doing. She was the one that acknowledged the challenges of using a wheelchair full time.

Her encouraging words, her words of wisdom, cracked something within me. I cried, not from pain, but from the exhaustion of pretending. Pretending I was fine. Pretending the cost was manageable. Pretending that independence meant doing everything the hardest way possible.

That night, I returned home and sat quietly. I stared at the wheelchair that I took with me in the back of my red convertible. I used it to go out to the car and a valet parker would assist me getting it into the car. It was the same way when I got home. I always travelled with my cane knowing that many of the places I needed to go would be inaccessible.

I had avoided the wheelchair. Avoided deciding what it meant. I kept glancing at it between half packed bags and unfinished thoughts, as if waiting for permission I already knew would not come from anyone else.

I did not feel brave. I felt tired of being at war with my own needs.

The First Roll

One morning, I pulled the red chair into the center of my living room. It looked smaller than it had in the corner, less threatening somehow, in the light.

I transferred into it cautiously, as though it might transform me the moment I sat down. As though I might become someone different, someone lesser.

But when I settled into the seat, adjusted the footrests, and placed my hands on the wheels, something unexpected happened. Nothing changed. I was still me, still Zully, still the designer, still the advocate, still the woman who loved bold colors and beautiful design.

What did change was the ease. I rolled across my apartment smoothly, efficiently, without pain. I reached my kitchen counter without exhaustion. I navigated to my studio without calculating energy reserves.

For the first time in years, movement didn't cost me everything.

I lived in a high-rise on the 14th floor with 24 hours security and valet parking. All the amenities inside the building allowed me to feel safe and secure about getting the assistance I needed when I decided to finally use my wheelchair on a full-time basis. I wanted to feel what it was like to see other people in the building outdoors in my neighborhood, seeing myself through their eyes and through what I imagined how they would think of me.

While testing the wheelchair and getting outside of my unit, I was confronted with carpeting. Using a wheelchair on carpeting wasn't easy. My arms struggled, so did my wrist muscles. Nevertheless, I proceeded towards the elevator. I'd never been taught how to enter an elevator. The ridges, the evenness from the carpeting to the entrance of the elevator, and maneuvering while people stood inside the elevator made me pause. What should I do? How do I manage this? How do I go? It was all a new experience, shocking and embarrassing to be seen struggling in the midst of a flood of people I didn't know.

I took the chair outside. People stared; of course they did. A woman in a bright red wheelchair attracted attention. But something had shifted in me. Their stares felt like their problem, not mine. The sidewalk stretched before me, and instead of seeing it as an obstacle course of energy expenditure, I saw it as an invitation. I rolled down the block, then around it. The autumn air felt different at this height, the world organized itself differently from this perspective.

However, the sidewalk was very misleading. Some things were not so visible, a slight unevenness in the paving could be immediately felt on the lower back or the trembling legs. The cracks every six feet whether filled with misguided pebbles or growing weeds could cause discomfort.

Although, as I rolled further down the sidewalk, something visceral woke up inside me; a memory of another red machine, another chapter of freedom. The sensation was unmistakable.

The red wheelchair became my red convertible. I think of young people driving red convertibles, feeling an air of freedom in the wind; free, independent, going wherever they want to go. That's what my red wheelchair represented. Not a medical device, not a symbol of limitation, but my vehicle for freedom and mobility. It was bold, it was visible, and it was mine.

It felt like being back in my Celica, windows down, music loud, wind tearing through my hair as the city rushed past me in streaks of light and motion. That car had been my first expression of defiance; I had shifted gears with the confidence of someone who refused to be contained.

And now, here it was again. That same fire. That same surge of aliveness. Only this time it came not from an engine but from me. From my hands on the wheels, from the open street before me, from the realization that speed was something I could generate, not something I had lost.

The red wheelchair glinted in the sunlight, and for the first time, I didn't see equipment. I saw acceleration. I saw heat. I saw a woman in motion.

The wind kissed my face, cool and electric. I was able to move faster. Though, managing a manual chair was challenging. Yes, managing with my head down, observing the cracks, the pedestrians, and down again to ensure that none of those cracks caused me to stumble and fall out of my chair wasn't easy.

But I was moving. I was free. And the chair wasn't confining me. It was freeing me.

Rediscovering the World

With the wheelchair, activities I'd given up became possible again. Museums, which had been exercises in exhaustion management, became places of genuine exploration. I could spend hours looking at art without calculating the cost of standing. Although living in the big city, I never ventured out alone. I would ask to be dropped off or go accompanied by my husband or friends.

Shopping transformed from an ordeal to an experience. I could browse, compare, and enjoy the process instead of rushing to complete it before my energy ran out.

Travel, which I'd loved but which had become increasingly difficult, opened up again. Airports, with their long distances and endless walking, became navigable. I learned about accessible travel, disability communities in different cities, the networks of knowledge that wheelchair users share.

One of my first trips was to a garden show. I'd always loved gardens but had struggled to navigate them with canes. The uneven terrain, the distances, the standing required to truly appreciate the plantings had all been too much.

But in my wheelchair, I could roll along the paths, pausing wherever something caught my eye. I could spend the entire day there, my energy devoted to appreciating beauty rather than managing mobility.

That day, an idea began to form: if gardens were difficult for me to access, how many other people were being excluded? What would a truly accessible garden look like, not one that grudgingly added wheelchair access as an afterthought, but one designed from the beginning to welcome all bodies?

I later learned there's a name for this: the 'curb-cut effect.' When accessibility improves for one group, everyone benefits. What helps a wheelchair user also helps a parent with a stroller, a traveler with luggage, a runner after injury.

Finding Community

I used to believe community meant gathering with people who shared your experiences. But growing up, I never had that. I wasn't part of disability camps or peer groups. I didn't trade stories in hospital waiting rooms or form friendships around shared equipment. I didn't even have the language to name what I was navigating.

My world, for a long time, was solitary. I knew how to adapt, how to push forward, how to survive but not how to belong.

So when I began using a wheelchair as an adult, the idea of "finding community" wasn't something I was seeking. I wasn't looking for peers. I wasn't searching for camaraderie. I had always been the one to carve my own way through unfamiliar terrain, and I assumed this chapter would be no different.

What surprised me was not friendship. It was recognition.

That was the nature of the "community" I encountered: not social, not emotional, but structural. A web of knowledge, advocacy, and lived wisdom that lived just beneath the surface of the city.

I didn't enter this community through friendship. I entered it through *need* through the practical, political, architectural realities of access. I learned which buildings had true ramps and which only pretended to. Which restrooms were accessible in name only. Which sidewalks dropped off suddenly. Which public events claimed inclusion but failed to deliver it.

I found myself absorbing information out of necessity, maps, shortcuts, mobility strategies, design flaws, and realizing I wasn't the only one taking mental notes. There was a quiet network of people all doing the same thing, not gathered together but moving through the same city with the same careful vigilance.

And eventually, advocacy pulled me closer.

I began attending meetings about access not because I wanted community, but because I wanted to always plan for what is to come into my future of mobility or lack thereof. Sitting in those rooms, I finally saw the true landscape of disability: not a cluster of lifelong friendships, but a coalition of people who refused to accept the limits placed upon them. People who believed in better architecture, better policy, better design. People who had spent their lives pushing against barriers and were ready for the next generation of solutions.

These weren't friends in the traditional sense. They were fellow architects of progress, voices that echoed mine, insisting the world could do better.

And surprisingly, that was its own kind of belonging. Not emotional intimacy, but shared purpose. Not social closeness, but a firm desire to create change.

Using a wheelchair didn't drop me into a ready-made social circle, it opened my eyes to a movement I hadn't known I was part of. A movement built not on shared childhoods or disability-centered bonding, but on the determination to transform the world into something more functional, more intelligent, more human.

The rehabilitation act in the US during the 70s served as a model for other countries to raise awareness toward people with disabilities.

Although, it was in the 90s when I became truly active. I became part of raising awareness of people with disabilities and the accommodations required. I found myself immersed into this new group of people that were very vocal. My being a somewhat quiet individual, I was more the conservative type. We used that balance to our advantage and that was how we succeeded in passing the Americans With Disabilities Act. Afterward, I was able to go to the United Nations to raise awareness on the rights of people with disabilities. I attended the habitat conference for humanity in Istanbul, Turkey, where I invited the 195 nations represented to make their respective embassies and consulates accessible. My wheelchair took me to all of these places where I never imagined. I found myself being the voice for those of us that were not out there in the world. My experience and my position allowed me to do that, to meet people that opened new doors and opportunities for me.

It was during this time that I became engaged with the women's movement, and also the rights of children. I went to China to the women's conference held in 1994 where persons with disabilities received a great deal of attention in a country that normally excluded them, particularly girls and women with disabilities.

The Garden Project

The idea that had sparked at the garden club grew into an obsession. I began researching accessible garden design, visiting sites, talking to landscape architects and occupational therapists.

Most "accessible" gardens I encountered were disappointing, a single paved path through an otherwise inaccessible space, designs that seemed to say "disabled people can use this small section while everyone else enjoys the real garden."

I wanted something different. I envisioned a garden where accessibility wasn't an accommodation but a foundation, where raised beds were designed at heights perfect for wheelchair users and standing gardeners alike, where paths were wide and smooth without looking institutional, where sensory experiences were available to people with diverse abilities.

I started small, creating a demonstration garden in my community. I used my design skills to make it beautiful as well as functional. The raised beds were constructed from warm wood, not cold metal. The plants were chosen for texture, scent, and visual appeal, engaging multiple senses.

Although an issue, we engaged volunteers to water regularly along with installing rain barrels. Plant labels included Braille. Seating areas were integrated throughout, not relegated to the margins.

When we opened the garden to the community, something beautiful happened. Yes, wheelchair users and people with other disabilities came and found it welcoming. But so did elderly visitors who appreciated the accessible seating. Parents with strollers enjoyed the smooth paths. Children loved the sensory elements that had been designed for blind visitors.

Universal design, I realized, benefits everyone. When you design for the margins, you often create something better for the center too.

The garden became a gathering place, a teaching site, a demonstration of what's possible when accessibility is central rather than peripheral. Other communities asked for consultation on their own accessible garden projects.

What had started as a personal need became a professional calling.

Designing that garden wasn't just about flowers or pathways, it was about creating in the world what I'd finally created within myself: access, dignity, and ease.

Redefining Independence

Perhaps the most profound lesson of wheelchair use was about independence itself.

For years, I'd defined independence as doing everything myself, needing no one, requiring no assistance. It was a deeply American definition, rooted in individualism and self-sufficiency.

But in the wheelchair community, I encountered a different understanding: interdependence.

Yes, I sometimes needed help with high shelves, with heavy doors, with stairs that had no alternative access. But accepting help didn't diminish me. And offering help to others in return, sharing information about accessible routes, advocating for better policies, using my design skills to improve access, created connection rather than dependency.

I learned to ask for help without shame. I learned that the problem wasn't my need for assistance but the barriers that created that need. I learned that true independence isn't about doing everything alone; it's about having the resources and support to live the life you choose.

Independence isn't about having no needs. It's about having control over how those needs are met.

I wasn't less independent because I used a wheelchair and sometimes needed assistance. I was actually more independent because I had the tools and community to live fully.

The Symbolism of Equipment

One afternoon, I sat in my studio surrounded by my collection of mobility devices. The crutches that had seen me through adolescence and young adulthood. The canes I'd decorated and designed. And now, the red wheelchair that had become my primary means of moving through the world.

Each device represented a chapter of my life, a stage of understanding, a different relationship with my body and my disability.

But looking at them together, I realized they weren't a progression of defeat; each one representing increased limitation. They were a progression of adaptation; each one representing a tool that gave me greater access to life.

The braces had helped me stand. The crutches had given my teenage self mobility. The canes had allowed me to navigate my career as a young professional. And the wheelchair? The wheelchair was giving me my life back.

Equipment, I understood, isn't about limitation. It's about possibility. And the question isn't "How disabled am I?" but rather "What tools do I need to live the life I want?"

Sometimes I think back to the first time I drove that red Celica onto the highway, the sun igniting the hood like a flame. I remember the way the engine hummed when I pressed the accelerator, how the world opened like a long invitation.

My wheelchair gives me that same sensation, different mechanics, same spirit. A forward pull. A widening horizon. A reminder that movement is still mine.

I may move differently now, but the fire is the same. The independence is the same. The freedom is the same.

Wheels are wheels. And when they're red, they burn a little brighter.

Some days, I still used my cane for short distances, for places where the wheelchair couldn't go, for moments when I chose walking despite the cost. The wheelchair didn't replace all my other options; it expanded them.

I could choose. That was the real freedom.

These tools didn't just change how I moved, they changed what I noticed.

The View from the Chair

From where I sit now, literally and metaphorically, the world looks different.

I notice different things: the lack of curb cuts, the inaccessible buildings, the assumptions embedded in how spaces are designed. But I also notice the beauty at this height, the details I missed when I was focused on just getting through the day, the people I might not have met if I hadn't joined this community.

The wheelchair changed my life, but not in the way I'd feared. It didn't confine me or define me or diminish me. It freed me to focus on what mattered: my work, my relationships, my advocacy, my creativity.

When people ask, and they always ask, "What happened?" I've learned to give different answers depending on my energy and their openness.

Sometimes I say simply, "I use a wheelchair for mobility."

Sometimes I say, "I have a condition that makes walking exhausting, so I use a chair to conserve energy for what matters."

And sometimes, when I sense genuine curiosity, I tell them what I wish everyone understood: "This wheelchair isn't a tragedy. It's a tool. And it's given me freedom I didn't have before."

The red convertible wasn't a surrender. It was a revolution.

And from this seat, I could finally see clearly enough to change not just my own life, but the systems and spaces that had limited so many others.

The chair didn't confine me; it expanded my world. This was freedom in motion, and I was finally moving toward the life I chose.

This was sitting down so I could finally stand up for something that mattered.

For families, the shift to a wheelchair often feels like a line crossed. For me, it was a door opened.

CHAPTER 8

REDEFINING FREEDOM THROUGH THE WHEELCHAIR

This is not a story about overcoming disability. This is a story about becoming myself fully, unapologetically, and on my own terms. The red wheelchair you'll see in these pages isn't a symbol of what I lost. It's a symbol of what I claimed.

The wheelchair is perhaps the most misunderstood piece of adaptive equipment in our cultural vocabulary. It serves as the universal symbol for disability appearing on parking signs, bathroom doors, and accessibility notices yet the reality of wheelchair use remains largely invisible to the non-disabled majority.

This gap between symbol and reality has profound consequences. It shapes how wheelchair users are perceived, how environments are designed, and how policies are crafted. Closing this gap requires understanding not just the mechanics of wheelchairs, but the social, psychological, and cultural dimensions of wheeled mobility.

This chapter redefines the wheelchair as a symbol of freedom, an innovation that expands human possibility rather than restricting it.

The Myth of "Confined to a Wheelchair"

Few phrases in disability discourse are as persistent or as damaging as "confined to a wheelchair" and its close cousin, "wheelchair-bound." These phrases appear regularly in news articles, medical literature, and everyday conversation. They reflect a fundamental misunderstanding of what wheelchairs actually do.

The Language Problem

The language we use to describe disability reveals underlying attitudes. Words like "confined" and "bound" suggest imprisonment, restriction, limitation. They frame the wheelchair as the problem rather than the solution.

But ask actual wheelchair users about their experience, and you'll hear a different story. Most describe their wheelchairs not as confining but as freeing, not as restrictions but as enablers. The wheelchair doesn't limit their movement; it facilitates it.

Consider the alternative: without a wheelchair, many users would be actually confined to their homes, to their beds, to spaces they could navigate with extreme difficulty and pain. The wheelchair is what allows them to go to work, attend school, travel, socialize, and participate in community life.

Disability activist Stella Young addressed this directly: "I use a wheelchair to get around. I'm not 'wheelchair-bound' any more than you're 'shoe-bound' because you wear shoes to walk." The comparison is apt: we don't describe ambulatory people as confined to their shoes, because we understand that shoes are tools that enable walking. Wheelchairs are tools that enable mobility.

Changing how we speak isn't cosmetic, it's foundational. Language sets the stage for how we design, include, and imagine accessibility itself.

Preferred Language

Disability community preferences have evolved toward language that emphasizes personhood and accurately describes function:

Preferred: "wheelchair user," "person who uses a wheelchair," or simply "disabled person".

Avoid: "confined to a wheelchair," "wheelchair-bound," "suffers from".

Preferred: "accessible parking".

Avoid: "handicapped parking".

Preferred: "disabled" or "has a disability".

Avoid: "handicapped," "differently-abled," "special needs".

Language matters because it shapes perception. When we describe wheelchair users accurately, as people using mobility tools, we open space for understanding that disability is about person-environment fit, not individual tragedy.

The Reality of Wheelchair Use

Wheelchair users are not a monolithic group. They include people with spinal cord injuries, multiple sclerosis, muscular dystrophy, chronic pain or fatigue conditions, elderly people who use wheelchairs to conserve energy, and people with temporary disabilities recovering from injury or surgery.

Many wheelchair users are also ambulatory; they can walk short distances but use wheelchairs for longer trips or to conserve energy. This "part-time" wheelchair use often confuses observers who carry a false assumption that wheelchair users cannot walk at all.

Research shows that approximately 65% of wheelchair users have some ambulatory ability. They make strategic decisions about when to walk and when to use wheels based on distance, energy, pain levels, and other factors. This flexibility is a strength, not an inconsistency that requires explanation.

This reality often surprises people because it challenges a deep-seated binary view of mobility: that one either walks or doesn't. In truth, most wheelchair users make dynamic, thoughtful choices based on energy, pain, and safety; a skillful adaptation, not a contradiction.

Two Ways of Understanding Wheelchairs

Understanding wheelchairs requires understanding two fundamentally different ways of thinking about disability: the medical model and the social model.

The Medical Model

The medical model, which has dominated healthcare and policy for centuries, locates disability in individual bodies. From this perspective, disability is a medical problem requiring treatment or cure, the goal is to make disabled people as "normal" as possible, and inability to participate is seen as resulting from bodily impairment.

Applied to wheelchairs, the medical model sees wheelchair use as a failure; a sign that medical interventions couldn't restore walking ability. The wheelchair is a last resort, a symbol of defeat.

The Social Model

The social model, developed by disability scholars and activists in the 1970s, locates disability not in bodies but in environments and attitudes. From this perspective, impairment (the bodily condition) is distinct from disability (the social barriers), disability results from the mismatch between body and environment, and inability to participate results from inaccessible design and discriminatory attitudes.

Applied to wheelchairs, the social model sees the chair as an effective mobility solution. The problem isn't the wheelchair; it's the stairs without ramps, the narrow doorways, the inaccessible bathrooms, and the attitudes that assume walking is superior to rolling.

In practice, wheelchair users live at the intersection of both models; negotiating the realities of their bodies and the barriers of their environments every day.

The Lived Reality

In practice, most wheelchair users hold a more integrated view. They acknowledge the reality of bodily impairment while recognizing that social barriers often create more limitations than their bodies do.

A wheelchair user might say: "Yes, my body has limitations. But the biggest barriers I face aren't my legs not working; they're buildings without ramps, people who stare, employers who assume I can't do the job, and a world designed without considering people like me."

This integrated perspective recognizes that disability emerges from the interaction between individual, environmental, and social factors. All three dimensions matter.

The Evolution of Wheelchair Design

Wheelchairs are highly engineered devices, and their design reveals important principles about human-centered design more broadly.

Early wheelchairs were heavy, institutional devices designed more for caregivers' convenience than users' autonomy. The traditional hospital wheelchair, chrome frame, vinyl seat, small front wheels, was designed to be pushed by someone else, not self-propelled.

When engineer and wheelchair athlete Ralf Hotchkiss began designing chairs with and for other users, he changed the field entirely. His lightweight, repairable designs became a model of user-led innovation, freedom not as theory, but as engineering.

The disability rights movement of the 1970s sparked a revolution in wheelchair design. Disabled designers and engineers began creating chairs that prioritized user autonomy, comfort, and performance. The result was the modern manual wheelchair: lightweight, maneuverable, customizable, and designed for active use.

Today's Options

Today's wheelchairs include:

Manual chairs: Self-propelled, available in sport, everyday, and ultra-lightweight versions.

Power chairs: Battery-operated with joystick or alternative controls.

Standing wheelchairs: Allow users to elevate to standing height.

Sport-specific chairs: Optimized for basketball, tennis, racing, etc.

All-terrain chairs: Designed for outdoor use with enhanced suspension and tires.

This reflects an important design principle: one size does not fit all. Different users need different solutions based on their bodies, lifestyles, and priorities.

Design Principles That Matter

Wheelchair design offers lessons applicable to all product design:

User-Centered Design: The best wheelchairs are designed with not just for users. Companies that employ wheelchair users as designers and testers ensure that lived experience informs technical specifications.

Customization: Bodies are different, and effective tools must accommodate that. Modern wheelchairs are highly adjustable, seat height, backrest angle, armrest position, footrest angle, and more can be customized to individual needs.

Performance vs. Medical Aesthetics: Early wheelchairs looked medical because they were designed by medical equipment companies. Contemporary wheelchairs often look like performance equipment, sleek, colorful, dynamic, because they're designed by and for active users.

Dignity Through Design: Good design respects users' dignity through proportions that look natural, colors and finishes that allow personal expression, and design language that conveys capability.

Context Awareness: Wheelchairs must function in diverse contexts: indoor/outdoor, smooth/rough terrain, narrow/wide spaces, cold/hot weather. Effective design considers the full range of use contexts.

Innovation in Action

Recent innovations demonstrate the potential of user-centered design:

- Smart wheelchairs that incorporate sensors, GPS, and AI to assist with navigation.
- Exoskeletons that allow some wheelchair users to stand and walk in controlled settings.
- Brain-computer interfaces that enable control through neural signals for users with limited movement.

- 3D-printed components that allow for rapid customization and repair.
- Adaptive seating that uses pressure mapping to prevent skin breakdown.
- Modular designs that allow users to switch between manual and power assist based on need.

These innovations emerge from understanding disability not as a problem to be solved but as a design challenge requiring creative solutions.

Building Environments That Work for Everyone

The quality of wheelchair design matters, but it's meaningless in inaccessible environments. True participation requires rethinking how we design spaces, establish policies, and structure activities.

Beyond Minimum Compliance

In the United States, the Americans with Disabilities Act (ADA) of 1990 established minimum accessibility standards for public spaces. These standards were revolutionary and necessary. But minimum compliance often produces grudging, minimal accessibility. The single ramp at the back entrance, the accessible bathroom on a different floor, the "special" accommodations that mark disabled people as exceptions.

Better accessibility goes beyond compliance to embrace universal design principles. Instead of asking "What's the minimum we must do?" it asks "How can we create spaces that work beautifully for everyone?"

What Good Accessibility Looks Like

Accessibility isn't a checklist, it's a mindset. It's the art of designing spaces, tools, and experiences that welcome everyone without needing an apology or workaround. Here's what meaningful accessibility truly looks like:

Integration, Not Segregation: Accessible routes and entrances should be primary, not secondary. When the main path is inclusive, no one has to ask for special permission to belong.

Dignity in Design: Accessibility features should be as aesthetically thoughtful as they are functional. Beauty and usability aren't opposites, they coexist when designers see inclusion as creativity, not compromise.

Multiple Means of Access: No single doorway, ramp, or format fits every need. Good design offers choices because access is about autonomy, not uniformity.

Built In, Not Added On: True accessibility isn't an afterthought or an adaptation. It's embedded from the start. When inclusivity is part of the design blueprint, it disappears into the experience naturally.

Beyond Physical Access: Accessibility extends beyond ramps and doors. It's also about emotional safety, sensory consideration, communication clarity, and digital inclusion. Freedom is holistic; it belongs in every dimension of design.

Examples That Get It Right

The Ed Roberts Campus (Berkeley, California): Named for disability rights pioneer Ed Roberts, this building was designed from inception to be radically accessible. Features include universal changing rooms with hoists, tactile wayfinding throughout, adjustable-height workstations in all offices, automated doors everywhere, seating options throughout for users with different needs, and a design aesthetic that's modern and beautiful, not institutional.

Well-Designed Community Spaces: Communities can implement accessibility principles without massive budgets. For community gardens, this means raised beds at wheelchair-accessible heights (24-30 inches), wide, firm paths between beds (minimum 36 inches, ideally 48+), vertical gardening options for users with different reach ranges, and shaded seating areas integrated throughout.

Universal Design Benefits Everyone

Understanding wheelchairs as methods of participation rather than symbols of limitation opens space for genuine inclusion. It also reveals that disability innovation benefits everyone:

- Curb cuts designed for wheelchairs help parents with strollers, travelers with luggage, and delivery workers with carts.
- Automated doors assist people carrying packages.
- Wide hallways benefit furniture movers and people who prefer personal space.
- Adjustable-height counters work for people of different heights.
- Clear signage helps everyone navigate unfamiliar spaces.

When we design for disability, we often create solutions that improve life for everyone. This is the promise of universal design: not special accommodations for a minority, but thoughtful design that recognizes every human as equal.

The Real Meaning of Freedom

The transformation in understanding wheelchairs from confining medical devices to freeing mobility tools reflects a broader shift in disability consciousness.

When we understand that wheelchairs enable rather than restrict, we start asking different questions. Instead of "How can we cure disability?" we ask "How can we design environments that work for diverse bodies?" Instead of "What's wrong with this person?" we ask "What's wrong with this building?"

This shift doesn't deny the reality of bodily impairment or the challenges of disability. It recognizes that many of those challenges are socially constructed and therefore socially solvable.

The wheelchair user who cannot enter a building isn't disabled by their wheelchair; they're disabled by the stairs. The wheelchair user who cannot participate in a meeting isn't limited by their mobility device; they're limited by the inaccessible venue choice.

The wheelchair is not a tragedy. It's a technology. And like all technologies, its effectiveness depends on the environment in which it operates and the attitudes of people who encounter it.

In accessible, welcoming environments, wheelchairs are simply one of many ways people move through the world. In inaccessible, discriminatory environments, wheelchairs become symbols of exclusion not because of what they are, but because of what we've failed to build.

Toolkit: What Adults Can Do Right Now

Understanding the social and emotional meaning of wheelchairs is only part of the journey. The next step is to act to help create a world where mobility tools are seen as symbols of agency, artistry, and inclusion. These tools will help adults, caregivers, and allies translate awareness into everyday advocacy.

What You Can Do Right Now:

Use empowering language. Replace phrases like "confined to a wheelchair" with "uses a wheelchair." Language either locks people in or opens doors, choose the latter.

Model curiosity, not pity. When children or peers ask questions, respond with calm openness. Curiosity builds understanding; pity teaches distance.

Learn about local resources. Inquire about places like Centers for Independent Living, adaptive sports programs, and disability advocacy organizations that support wheelchair users.

Ask before assisting. Always ask, "Would you like help with that?" instead of assuming. True respect begins with autonomy.

Advocate for accessible design. Point out barriers in schools, workplaces, and public areas. Stairs without ramps, narrow doorways, or poor signage. Naming a problem is the first step to fixing it.

Celebrate design and identity. Share stories or examples of wheelchair users who embody freedom and creativity, athletes, artists, inventors. Representation shifts perception.

Invite inclusion. In community settings, ensure social events, group activities, and public programs are accessible from the start, not adjusted later as an afterthought.

Daily Habits That Help:

Small, consistent actions create lasting change. Here's how to bring inclusion into daily rhythm:

- **Notice your environment.** Each day, identify one space, home, office, park, or store, that could be more inclusive. What small change would help?
- **Language check-ins.** If you hear outdated or pitying phrases, gently reframe them. Use calm corrections that teach without shaming.
- **Pause before judgment.** When you see a wheelchair user walking briefly or transferring, remind yourself: mobility is complex. There's no single story of ability.

- **Share positive examples.** Post or talk about inclusive design innovations, accessible art, or mobility pride online. Visibility inspires normalization.
- **Reflect at day's end.** Ask yourself, "Did I make inclusion easier for someone today or harder?" Let that reflection guide tomorrow's choices.

What to Watch For:

Freedom through design is a community effort and sometimes, exclusion happens quietly. Watch for these moments:

- **Unintentional segregation.** "Accessible" events or entrances separated from the main flow signal token inclusion. Speak up for integration.
- **Overhelping.** Jumping in without asking may seem kind but often undermines autonomy. Empower before assisting.
- **Invisibility in design discussions.** If disability voices are absent from policy, architecture, or leadership meetings, accessibility will always be incomplete.
- **Pity disguised as praise.** Compliments like "You're so inspiring" can reduce someone's life to a symbol. Instead, appreciate skill, humor, creativity, things that affirm humanity, not hierarchy.

If you notice these issues, create opportunities for honest conversation, connect the person with disability community and resources, and work to address environmental and attitudinal barriers that contribute to their struggles.

How to Keep Perspective:

You don't need to fix everything; you only need to start seeing differently. Change begins with attention: to language, to space, to dignity. Each thoughtful question or design choice ripples outward into a culture where wheelchairs are not symbols of loss but of freedom, artistry, and belonging.

Inclusion isn't a favor; it's a shared right. And every act of awareness, no matter how small, strengthens that right for everyone.

Key Takeaway:

Freedom isn't about walking. It's about access. The wheelchair is not a boundary but a bridge, a tool that transforms limits into landscapes of possibility. When we design with empathy and act with awareness, we don't just build ramps; we build belonging.

PART V
Leadership from the Margins

CHAPTER 9

UNDERSTANDING EMPOWERMENT LEADERSHIP THROUGH LIVED EXPERIENCE

The conventional wisdom about leadership suggests that effective leaders are those who overcome obstacles, who don't let challenges slow them down, who power through adversity. But this model misunderstands the relationship between limitation and leadership capacity.

This chapter argues that disability experience, far from limiting leadership potential, develops the very competencies today's complex world demands: adaptability, empathy, and systemic innovation.

The most effective leaders aren't those who've faced the fewest obstacles, they're often those who've navigated the most complex constraints. And people with disabilities, who've spent their lives adapting to barriers and creating innovative solutions, often possess leadership capabilities that others must work years to develop.

Understanding this requires rethinking what leadership is, how it develops, and what qualities make leaders truly effective in complex, diverse environments.

Leadership Lessons from Disability Experience

Disability experience develops specific competencies that are essential for effective leadership. These aren't compensations for limitations. They're capabilities that emerge from navigating complex challenges.

Empathy and Emotional Intelligence

Empathy, the ability to understand and share the feelings of others is consistently identified as a crucial leadership quality. Research shows that empathetic leaders build stronger teams, achieve better outcomes, and create more innovative organizations.

People with disabilities often develop heightened empathy through direct experience of marginalization, exclusion, and misunderstanding. When you've been stereotyped, underestimated, or dismissed because of visible difference, you become acutely sensitive to how others might feel when treated similarly.

Studies show that people with disabilities score significantly higher on measures of empathetic concern and perspective-taking than matched non-disabled groups. This isn't because disability inherently creates empathy, but because the social experience of disability navigating a world not designed for you develops empathetic capacity.

This empathy translates directly into leadership effectiveness. Disabled leaders often excel at:

Reading social dynamics: Understanding unspoken hierarchies and power relationships.

Recognizing exclusion: Identifying when people feel marginalized or unheard.

Creating psychological safety: Building environments where people feel comfortable being authentic.

Valuing diverse contributions: Recognizing that different doesn't mean deficient.

These skills are invaluable in diverse organizations where leaders must navigate cultural differences, power dynamics, and competing priorities.

Strategic Planning and Systems Thinking

When planning and coordinating travel missions for my nonprofit organization to Latin America, I made plans for the volunteer team. For me, it required a different sort of organizing. I was the disabled leader going into villages or islands that would be totally inaccessible, experiencing unexpected situations, not only for the team, but for myself.

When you use adaptive equipment, every activity requires planning. You must consider route accessibility, energy expenditure, equipment functionality, time requirements, backup plans for when standard approaches fail, and environmental factors like weather, terrain, and crowds.

This constant planning develops what organizational theorists call "strategic thinking" the ability to anticipate challenges, consider multiple scenarios, and develop contingency plans.

Disabled leaders often bring this planning rigor to organizations. They anticipate obstacles others miss, develop detailed implementation plans, create backup strategies, think systematically about how components interconnect, and consider edge cases and exceptions.

Disability advocate Haben Girma, who is both deaf and blind, describes how navigating the world with her disabilities developed her ability to "think three steps ahead, always planning for what might go wrong and how to adapt." This forward-thinking is precisely what organizations need in complex, rapidly changing environments.

Strategic thinking and perspective-taking are twin competencies. Where strategic planning manages systems, perspective-taking manages people understanding not only how processes intersect, but how human experiences shape those intersections.

Perspective-Taking and Problem-Solving

People with disabilities routinely practice perspective-taking imagining how situations appear from different vantage points. When a building is inaccessible, you must think from the architect's perspective (why was it designed this way?), the business owner's perspective (what would make them prioritize accessibility?), and the policy maker's perspective (what regulations could require change?).

This multi-perspective thinking develops cognitive flexibility and the ability to shift between different frameworks and approaches.

Disabled leaders often demonstrate:

- **Ability to reframe problems**: Seeing challenges from multiple angles.
- **Comfort with ambiguity**: Recognizing that situations may not have single right answers.
- **Innovation under constraint**: Finding creative solutions when standard approaches don't work.
- **Cultural competence**: Understanding how different groups experience the same situation differently.

The same mental flexibility that enables empathy also fuels innovation, the ability to imagine different paths when the usual ones are blocked.

How Constraints Create Innovation

The relationship between constraint and innovation is well-documented in creativity research. When standard approaches aren't available, people develop novel solutions. When resources are limited, they create more efficient processes. When obstacles block the obvious path, they discover alternative routes.

The Innovation Connection

For people with disabilities, this innovation isn't optional; it's necessary for daily function. Consider these examples:

Communication Innovation: Deaf communities developed sign languages that are linguistically complex and culturally rich. Text messaging and video calling, now used globally, were driven significantly by deaf users' communication needs.

Mobility Innovation: Wheelchair users pioneered techniques for navigating obstacles that influenced robotics and autonomous vehicle design.

Information Access Innovation: Blind computer users drove development of screen readers, which led to voice-activated technology now used in smart speakers, navigation systems, and hands-free devices.

Design Innovation: Universal design principles emerged from disability advocacy and now influence everything from architecture to software development to consumer products.

Globally, the same pattern holds. Japan's tactile paving, designed by Seiichi Miyake, who was partially sighted, now guides millions of travelers worldwide. What began as an accessibility solution became a universal navigation language.

The Adaptability Advantage

Beyond specific innovations, disability experience develops general adaptability, the capacity to adjust effectively to changing circumstances.

People with disabilities practice this cycle constantly: noticing when an environment or situation isn't working for your needs, adjusting approach (finding alternative routes, requesting accommodations, using different equipment), and building knowledge about what works in different contexts.

This practiced adaptability makes disabled leaders particularly effective in volatile, uncertain, complex, and ambiguous environments, exactly the conditions modern organizations face.

Reframing Disability Inclusion as Strategic Advantage

Traditional approaches to disability in organizations frame inclusion as moral obligation or legal compliance. But disability access is actually a strategic advantage that improves organizational performance.

These outcomes aren't coincidental; they're the same competencies cultivated through disability experience: empathy, adaptability, and innovation at scale.

The Evidence for Inclusion

Research consistently shows that disability-inclusive organizations outperform less accessible competitors:

Innovation: Companies with cultures of belonging are 1.7 times more likely to be innovation leaders in their markets.

Problem-Solving: Diverse teams, including disability representation, solve problems faster and more accurately than homogeneous teams.

Market Access: The disability market (disabled people and their families and friends) represents over $8 trillion in global spending power.

Employee Performance: Accessible companies have higher cash flow per employee and are more likely to outperform industry peers.

Retention: Organizations with strong disability inclusion programs have lower turnover and higher employee engagement.

Universal Design in Organizations

Just as universal design creates physical environments that work for diverse bodies, organizations can apply these principles to policies, practices, and culture:

Fair Use: Policies that work for everyone, no "special" exceptions needed.

Flexibility: Offer multiple ways to achieve results, respecting varied work styles.

Simple and Intuitive: Keep systems transparent; clarity is inclusion.

Perceptible Information: Communicate across visual, auditory, and written channels.

Tolerance for Error: Create safe spaces for experimentation and learning.

Low Physical Effort: Streamline unnecessary demands, meetings, forms, bureaucracy.

Space for Diversity: Provide physical and psychological room for difference.

Building Inclusive Family Culture

The principles that make organizations more inclusive also make families stronger. Parents can apply disability leadership lessons to create family cultures that value innovation and authentic participation.

One parent I spoke with described how their family approached a weekend hike. Together, they mapped trails, adjusted pacing, and built rest stops into the route. What began as a logistical challenge became a lesson in leadership, each member contributing ideas, empathy, and adaptability.

Teaching Leadership at Home

Model empathy by acknowledging others' feelings and perspectives, especially when they differ from your own.

Practice planning by involving children in thinking through accessibility needs for family activities, teaching strategic thinking early.

Celebrate creative problem-solving when children find innovative ways to participate or adapt activities to their needs.

Value diverse contributions by recognizing that family members contribute in different ways, all of which are valuable.

Normalize asking for help by demonstrating that requesting support is a strength, not a weakness.

Create psychological safety where family members can express authentic feelings without judgment.

Building Advocacy Skills

Children with disabilities who grow up in families that treat them as capable problem-solvers develop strong self-advocacy skills. Adults can foster this by:

- Involving children in accommodation decisions at age-appropriate levels.
- Teaching them to articulate their needs clearly.
- Practicing responses to common questions or challenges.
- Connecting them with disabled adult mentors who model advocacy.
- Celebrating their innovations and adaptations.
- Trusting their assessment of what they need.

Toolkit: What Adults Can Do Right Now

Understanding empowerment through lived experience isn't just about awareness; it's about rethinking how we define leadership itself. This toolkit invites you to apply disability-informed wisdom to your daily life, leadership, and relationships. Whether you lead a team, a classroom, a family, or a community, these practices help you model inclusion as a living, breathing habit, not a one-time initiative.

What You Can Do Right Now:

Redefine leadership. See leadership not as hierarchy, but as collaboration. Ask: *How can I create space for others to contribute their strengths?*

Audit your decision-making. When making plans, pause and ask, *Who isn't represented here? Who might experience this differently?* Inclusion begins with noticing absence.

Value adaptation as intelligence. Instead of viewing adjustments or workarounds as "special," celebrate them as signs of creative problem-solving. Adaptive thinkers make systems better for everyone.

Share power early. Invite voices into projects from the start, not just for review at the end. Participation is power; inclusion after the fact is repair.

Redefine 'efficiency.' True efficiency includes sustainability and wellbeing. Leadership rooted in accessibility often moves slower but it lasts longer.

For Parents Specifically:

Cultivate leadership at home by giving your child real responsibilities and decision-making power appropriate to their age.

Connect them with disabled adult mentors who can model successful navigation of disability in adulthood.

Teach self-advocacy by involving your child in their own accommodation planning and medical decisions.

Celebrate their innovations when they find creative solutions to challenges.

Build disability pride by connecting with the disability community and culture, not just medical professionals.

Challenge low expectations from schools, family members, or others who underestimate your child's potential.

Model authentic vulnerability by being honest about your own struggles and showing that asking for help is natural.

Create space for all emotions about disability including frustration, anger, and sadness while also celebrating capability and possibility.

Daily Habits That Help:

Small, consistent habits make inclusion instinctive rather than performative. These micro-practices rewire how we think about difference, access, and leadership presence.

- **Ask better questions.** Start every meeting with: "What do you need to participate fully today?"
- **Model flexibility.** Adjust processes to fit people, not people to fit processes.
- **Pause before reacting.** When something feels "inefficient," ask if the system, not the person, is what needs to adapt.
- **Make learning visible.** Share how you adapt in real time; normalize problem-solving out loud.
- **End your day with reflection.** Ask: "Did I create more access today than yesterday?" Let that question become your quiet metric for leadership growth.

What to Watch For:

Empowerment grows strongest when we identify the invisible habits that hold old systems in place. Watch for these moments. They're small, but they shape entire cultures.

- **The language of permission.** If you catch yourself saying "allow" or "let," reframe it. Empowerment isn't about permission. It's about participation.
- **The myth of independence.** Independence is valuable, but interdependence is what sustains communities. Leadership thrives in networks, not silos.
- **Unconscious gatekeeping.** When you think, *they wouldn't be comfortable with this*, pause. You might be deciding for someone else instead of inviting them in.

- **Inclusion by invitation.** If participation depends on someone being invited, it's not yet systemic. Work toward default access where everyone can enter, speak, and belong without extra effort.
- **Emotional burnout.** When inclusion work feels exhausting, it's often because the system still resists it. Rest is part of resistance; leadership requires recovery, not martyrdom.

How to Keep Perspective:

Empowerment isn't a finish line; it's a rhythm. Some days you'll feel like a bridge-builder; other days, you'll feel like you're standing alone in the gap. Both moments are essential.

Key Takeaway:

Empowerment begins where control ends. When you stop leading from authority and start leading from access, you transform leadership itself. Disability-informed insight teaches that strength is not in dominance. It's in design, trust, and interdependence.

CHAPTER 10

FROM PITY TO PARTNERSHIP: CREATING REAL INCLUSION

Disability awareness campaigns have taught people that disability exists. Buildings display the international symbol of access. Organizations host disability awareness months. All types of stories circulate on social media. We are more aware of disability than ever before.

Yet awareness without action is performance. It allows organizations to claim commitment to inclusion while maintaining exclusionary practices. It enables individuals to feel good about their enlightened attitudes while doing nothing to remove barriers.

This chapter explores how we move beyond symbolic gestures to build systems grounded in commitment to change, application and enforcement of policies, and universal design.

True inclusion requires moving beyond awareness to substantive action, guided by universal design principles, and led by disabled people themselves.

Awareness: Understanding the Language of Inclusion

Language shapes how we think, and how we think shapes what we do. The evolution of disability language reflects changing understandings of what disability is and what inclusion requires.

From Medical Terminology to Identity Language

Early disability language emerged from medical contexts: patients, sufferers, invalids, crippled, handicapped. This language positioned disability as pathology requiring treatment, cure, or charitable assistance.

The disability rights movement introduced person-first language in the 1980s: "person with a disability" rather than "disabled person." The intent was to emphasize personhood over diagnosis, to resist reduction to medical conditions.

But person-first language has limitations. It suggests that disability is separate from the person, something they "have" rather than an identity they embody. For many disabled people, disability isn't an accessory to be distinguished from selfhood, it's integral to who they are.

This led to identity-first language: "disabled person," "blind person," "autistic person." This approach asserts disability as a legitimate identity, not a tragic circumstance to be minimized.

Current best practice recognizes that preferences vary. Some prefer person-first language; others prefer identity-first; many use both depending on context. The key is asking individuals their preference rather than assuming.

As language evolved, so did the stories we tell about disability, and those stories have shaped public perception just as powerfully as any term or label.

From Inspiration to Authentic Representation

Traditional disability narratives positioned disabled people as inspirational objects, people whose main social function is to make non-disabled people feel grateful or motivated.

Activist Stella Young famously critiqued this "inspiration porn."

Inspiration Porn is used to describe the objectification of disabled people with the intention of making people without disabilities feel good. The term was made popular by Stella Young, a disabled comedian and activist, in her TED Talk titled "I'm Not Your Inspiration, Thank You Very Much." Young explained that society has been sold the lie that having a disability is a bad thing, so simply living with a disability makes someone exceptional. The media tends to glorify disabled people for existing and praise non-disabled people for helping disabled people. These superficial narratives have detrimental effects on the representation and perception of disabled people in society.

Young argued that disabled people are not here for non-disabled people's benefit. We are not inspiring for doing ordinary things. We are not brave for existing. We are not tragic heroes overcoming our limitations.

The shift is toward authentic representation: disabled people as complex characters in media, as experts consulted in our own right, as leaders making decisions, as ordinary people living ordinary lives.

This means:

In media: Disabled characters with story arcs unrelated to their disabilities, playing diverse roles, portrayed by disabled actors.

In workplaces: Disabled people in leadership positions, making strategic decisions, valued for professional expertise.

In education: Disability history and culture in curriculum, disabled educators teaching all subjects.

In policy: Disabled people leading disability policy initiatives, not just advising from margins.

Key Terminology for Respectful Communication

Understanding disability language requires precision, context, and respect. These categories help readers navigate terminology with clarity and intention.

1. Mobility-Related Terminology

- **Wheelchair user** – A person who uses a wheelchair. Avoid "wheelchair-bound."
- **Mobility device** – Includes walkers, canes, scooters, braces; a neutral, inclusive term.
- **Ambulatory / non-ambulatory** – Describes mobility, not capability.
- **Transfers** – Moving from one surface to another (e.g., chair to bed).

Use: Disabled person / person with a disability (based on individual preference), wheelchair user / person who uses a wheelchair. Avoid: Wheelchair-bound, confined to a wheelchair.

Avoid: Handicapped, crippled, invalid, differently-abled, special needs, wheelchair-bound, confined to a wheelchair.

2. Sensory Disability Terminology

- **Blind / low vision** – Use based on the individual's preference; avoid euphemisms like "visually impaired" unless self-identified.
- **Deaf / hard of hearing** – "Deaf" may refer to identity and culture; "hard of hearing" describes partial hearing loss.

- **ASL user** – A person whose primary language is American Sign Language.

Use: Blind person / person who is blind, deaf person / person who is deaf.

Avoid: Suffering from blindness, vision-impaired (unless clinically accurate), hearing-impaired, deaf and dumb.

3. Cognitive, Learning & Neurodiversity Terms

- **Autistic person / person with autism** – Respect identity-first or person-first based on the individual's choice.
- **Neurodivergent** – Someone whose cognitive processing differs from typical patterns.
- **Intellectual disability** – Preferred over outdated terms like "mental retardation."
- **Dyslexia / dyscalculia / ADHD** – Specific, accurate terms for distinct needs.

4. Mental & Psychiatric Disability Terms

- **Psychiatric disability** – Neutral term acknowledging diagnoses without stigma.
- **Mental health condition** – Can be used interchangeably depending on context.
- **Crisis plan** – A plan developed collaboratively for safety and support.

Use: Person with mental illness / person with psychiatric disability.

Avoid: Crazy, insane, psycho, mentally ill (as noun).

5. General Etiquette & Interaction Language

- **Person-first language** – "Person with..." used when preferred by the individual.

- **Identity-first language** – "Disabled person..." used when preferred as a statement of pride.
- **Access needs** – What someone requires to participate fully (e.g., captioning).
- **Accommodation vs. modification** – "Accommodation" supports access; "modification" changes the task itself.
- **Care partner** – More respectful alternative to "caretaker" or "caregiver."
- **Support animal / service animal** – Use precisely; don't interchange.

Use: Non-disabled person, accessible parking, accessible bathroom.

Avoid: Normal person, healthy person, able-bodied (when referring to mental/sensory disabilities), handicapped parking, disabled bathroom (the bathroom isn't disabled).

Action: Universal Design Principles in Practice

Universal design creating environments and products usable by the widest range of people offers a practical framework for moving from awareness to action.

The Seven Principles Applied to Real Contexts

Developed by Ronald Mace and colleagues, these principles apply across contexts:

Principle 1: Fair Use

Design is useful to people with a wide range of abilities.

Why it matters: When systems are designed for more than one "typical" user, they reduce barriers for everyone.

Examples:

- **Workplace:** All documents and training materials are available in accessible digital formats.
- **School:** Students receive materials in multiple formats (text, audio, visual).
- **Community:** Public buildings maintain step-free entrances with clear signage.

Principle 2: Flexibility in Use

Design accommodates individual preferences, abilities, and learning styles.

Why it matters: Flexibility invites participation by allowing people to engage in the ways that work best for them.

Examples:

- **Workplace:** Employees choose between in-person, remote, or hybrid meeting formats.
- **School:** Students can demonstrate learning through written, oral, or project-based work.
- **Community:** Public services offer online, phone, and in-person access.

Principle 3: Simple and Intuitive Use

Design is easy to understand, regardless of experience or cognitive ability.

Why it matters: The less effort required to interpret a system, the more inclusive and effective it becomes.

Examples:

- **Workplace:** Onboarding instructions use plain language and visual guides.
- **School:** Classrooms display clear, predictable routines with visual schedules.

- **Community:** Voting instructions use step-by-step diagrams and simplified wording.

Principle 4: Perceptible Information

Information is presented in multiple ways to ensure it can be understood by everyone.

Why it matters: People can only participate when essential information is communicated across sensory modes.

Examples:

- **Workplace:** Announcements are provided as audio, text, and email.
- **School:** Fire alarms include both sound and flashing lights.
- **Community:** Transit systems use high-contrast signage with universal symbols.

Principle 5: Tolerance for Error

Design minimizes hazards and negative consequences from accidental actions.

Why it matters: Systems that anticipate mistakes reduce harm and make participation safer and more confident.

Examples:

- **Workplace:** Software offers clear “undo” functions and autosave.
- **School:** Lab spaces include clear safety zones and adaptive equipment.
- **Community:** Crosswalks include extended timing and curb-level refuge islands.

Principle 6: Low Physical Effort

Design allows efficient use with minimal fatigue.

Why it matters: Reducing physical strain increases access for disabled people and benefits everyone from children to older adults.

Examples:

- **Workplace:** Doors open automatically; workstations offer adjustable furniture.
- **School:** Classrooms are arranged to allow easy movement between spaces.
- **Community:** Public parks include flat, smooth pathways for wheelchair and stroller access.

Principle 7: Size and Space for Approach and Use

Design provides adequate space for posture, mobility devices, and varied interaction styles.

Why it matters: Space determines whether people can not only enter but navigate, stay, and contribute meaningfully.

Examples:

- **Workplace:** Meeting rooms include wide pathways and varied seating options.
- **School:** Desks and tables allow wheelchair users and students with mobility needs to participate equally.
- **Community:** Public restrooms include stalls wide enough for mobility devices and caregiver assistance.

Implementing Universal Design: A Phased Approach

Universal design becomes most effective when organizations treat it as an ongoing system, not a one-time retrofit. A phased approach helps ensure that accessibility isn't just implemented but maintained.

Organizations can implement universal design systematically:

Phase 1: Assessment Audit current environments, policies, and practices. Identify barriers across disability types. Gather input from disabled employees, students, or community members.

Phase 2: Prioritization Address barriers preventing participation first. Consider impact (number of people affected) and feasibility. Plan for both immediate fixes and long-term improvements.

Phase 3: Implementation Make changes starting with highest-priority items. Build accessibility into new initiatives from the start. Train staff on universal design principles.

Phase 4: Evaluation Gather feedback from users. Measure participation and satisfaction. Adjust based on real-world experience.

Phase 5: Sustainability Integrate universal design into standard operating procedures. Include accessibility in all planning processes. Maintain commitment through leadership changes.

Accountability: Strategies for Creating Real Change

Different roles require different strategies for advancing inclusion.

For Educators

Universal Design for Learning (UDL)

UDL provides a framework for accessible education:

Multiple Means of Representation: Present information in varied formats, visual, auditory, and tactile learning materials; text with images, diagrams, and videos; adjustable text size, color contrast, and audio speed.

Multiple Means of Action and Expression: Allow varied ways to demonstrate knowledge, written essays, oral presentations, visual projects, performances; use of assistive technology as needed; choice in how to show learning.

Multiple Means of Engagement: Provide varied ways to motivate and engage, connect to students' interests and experiences; offer choices in topics and approaches; build community and collaboration opportunities.

Accessible Classroom Practices

- **Proactive accommodation**: Offer support to all students rather than waiting for disclosure.
- **Flexible deadlines**: Allow extensions when needed without penalty.
- **Clear communication**: Provide syllabi, assignments, and expectations in accessible formats.
- **Representation**: Include disability in curriculum across subjects.
- **Language**: Use respectful language and challenge language that reinforces negative assumptions about disability.

Partnership with Families

Communicate regularly about student progress and needs. Listen to family expertise about their child. Collaborate on goals and strategies. Respect cultural differences in understanding disability.

For Healthcare Providers

Accessible Clinical Practice

- **Accessible facilities**: Ensure exam tables, scales, and equipment accommodate diverse bodies.
- **Communication access**: Provide interpreters, written materials, visual aids as needed.
- **Time**: Allow adequate appointment time for communication and care.
- **Whole person care**: Address health concerns beyond disability.
- **Cultural competence**: Understand disability culture and community.

Patient-Centered Care

- **Ask, don't assume**: Inquire about the patient's needs and preferences.
- **Respect expertise**: Recognize patients as experts in their own bodies.
- **Shared decision-making**: Collaborate on treatment plans.
- **Address barriers**: Consider social determinants of health affecting access to care.

When healthcare becomes accessible, it does more than treat illness, it builds trust. And trust is the foundation of any system that aims to care for the whole person.

For Advocates and Allies

Advocates and allies play a critical role in advancing disability awareness, but effective support requires clarity of purpose and an understanding of where influence begins. Your work starts by recognizing who should lead, then addressing the systems that shape people's lives, and finally moving into coalition building, consistent action, and the humility required to do this work well.

1. Center Disabled Leadership

Follow the lead of disabled people whose expertise, lived experience, and insight drive the movement. Leadership should be informed by those directly impacted.

2. Address Systems

Identify inequities in policy, infrastructure, culture, and organizational decision-making. Use your influence to challenge systemic barriers rather than only responding to individual incidents.

3. Build Coalitions

Work with community groups, cross-disability partners, educators, organizations, and other allies. Sustainable change happens through shared effort and responsibility.

4. Take Consistent Action

Advocacy is not symbolic; it is daily, ongoing work. Speak up, intervene, offer support, amplify disabled voices, and keep showing up even when it is uncomfortable or inconvenient.

5. Practice Humility and Learning

Remain open, teachable, and accountable. Accept feedback, apologize without defensiveness, and recognize that allyship is a lifelong learning process.

Toolkit: What You Can Do Right Now

Understanding shifts perspective; but daily communication is where transformation happens. These tools help you turn the concepts in this chapter into actions that build trust, reduce harm, and strengthen every relationship.

What You Can Do Right Now:

Use these immediate practices to ground your communication in clarity, respect, and consent.

- **Ask before you engage emotionally or personally.** Begin with: "Is this a good time?" or "How would you like to talk about this?" Consent is the foundation of respectful dialogue.
- **Name access needs out loud, yours and theirs.** Try: "Do you need more time, another format, or a different way of speaking about this?" Normalizing access requests reduces pressure for everyone.

- **Use precise, non-euphemistic disability language.** Replace vagueness ("special needs," "challenged") with accurate terms that honor lived experience and identity.
- **Mirror the language someone uses for themselves.** If they say "I'm autistic," follow their lead. If they say "I'm a person with PTSD," reflect that choice.
- **Model steady, grounded communication in high-stakes moments.** Your calm tone becomes permission for the other person to stay regulated.
- **Validate before you problem-solve.** Phrases like "That makes sense" or "I hear you" build safety and prevent defensiveness.
- **Practice repair quickly and directly.** If you misspeak, say: "Thank you for telling me. Let me try again." Repair builds more trust than perfection.
- **Offer multiple ways to participate in conversations.** Some people communicate best through text, writing, visuals, or asynchronous responses.
- **Honor silence.** Non-response is information, not a failure. Give people time to process.
- **Use plain language when stakes are high.** Short sentences, clear meaning, and unambiguous requests reduce risk and increase clarity.

Daily Habits That Help:

True communication skill develops in the quiet routines of everyday life. The following habits strengthen connection and help people feel safe, seen, and respected.

- **Check in regularly without assumptions.** "How has communication been feeling for you recently?" invites clarity and honesty.

- **Use reflective language.** Instead of "Good point," try: "I appreciate the clarity you brought to that thought," or "Your perspective helped me understand this differently."
- **Normalize access conversations.** Ask in low-stakes moments: "How do you prefer to receive information?"
- **Slow your pacing.** Speaking 10–20% slower makes conversations more accessible and lowers emotional heat.
- **Use trauma-informed phrasing.** Replace "Calm down" with "Take your time"; replace "Why didn't you" with "Help me understand what happened."
- **Build emotional vocabulary together.** Terms like "overwhelm," "activation," or "shutdown" help group conversations become more intentional and less reactive.
- **Practice environmental accessibility.** Dim the lights, reduce background noise, or offer written notes without waiting to be asked.
- **Celebrate moments of clarity and connection.** When someone articulates a need or boundary, affirm it: "Thank you for telling me. That helps me show up better."
- **Revisit conversations when needed.** Saying, "Can we return to this tomorrow?" shows respect for processing time.
- **Use daily affirmations of dignity.** Simple reminders "Your needs matter," "Your voice is important" teach people to trust their own experience.

What to Watch For:

Communication struggles often signal deeper access, emotional, or relational needs. These patterns are not "problems" they are information guiding you toward better support.

- **Frequent misunderstandings or misinterpretations.** → May indicate unclear language, processing differences, or emotional overwhelm.
- **Avoidance of conversations or consistent withdrawal.** → Often a sign that communication feels unsafe, rushed, or too demanding.
- **Emotional shutdowns, blank stares, or monotone responses.** → Signals cognitive overload, sensory strain, or a need for slower pacing.
- **Escalation during small disagreements.** → Suggests unspoken fear, previous harm, or unclear boundaries.
- **Repeated "I don't know" responses.** → Can indicate shutdown, masking, or difficulty processing questions in real time.
- **Heightened sensitivity to tone or phrasing**. → Often connected to trauma history, chronic marginalization, or high-stakes topics.
- **Difficulty articulating needs, even when they trust you.** → Signals a need for structured prompts, written options, or more processing time.

If you notice these patterns, don't assume resistance, avoidance, or emotional immaturity. See them as data, an invitation to adjust your approach, slow the pace, clarify expectations, or check on access needs. Collaborative communication can repair more than any single strategy.

How to Keep Perspective:

No one communicates perfectly, especially across differences in disability, culture, trauma history, or emotional wiring. What matters most is your willingness to stay present, patient, and curious. Some conversations will feel smooth; others may feel tangled or exhausting. Both are understandable.

When you practice self-compassion, you model the very thing this chapter teaches:

Communication is not about flawless execution. It's about staying connected even when it's imperfect.

On hard days, remind yourself:

- Communication is a skill, not a moral measure.
- Everyone has moments of overwhelm or misunderstanding.
- Repair is always possible.
- Progress is rarely linear, but it is always meaningful.

Your steadiness becomes the safety that allows others to speak openly. Your patience becomes the bridge to mutual understanding. And your willingness to keep learning becomes the most powerful tool of all.

For Educators:

- **Use Universal Design for Learning** by providing materials in multiple formats, offering choice in assignments, and creating flexible assessment options.
- **Create proactive accommodations** by making supports available to all students without requiring disclosure of disability.
- **Include disability in curriculum** across subjects: disability history, disabled authors and scientists, disability perspectives on current events.
- **Use respectful language** and address language rooted in stereotypes about disability when you hear it from students or colleagues.
- **Partner with families** by listening to their expertise, communicating regularly, and collaborating on goals.

- **Make your classroom physically accessible** with adequate circulation space, flexible seating, and materials at various heights.
- **Build a community** that celebrates inclusion and challenges bullying or exclusion based on disability.
- **Connect students with disabled role models** through guest speakers, literature, and media representation.

For Healthcare Providers:

- **Ensure physical accessibility** of your facility, exam rooms, and equipment.
- **Provide communication access** through interpreters, written materials, visual aids, and adequate time.
- **Ask patients about their needs** rather than making assumptions based on visible disability.
- **Address the whole person**, not just the disability, and recognize patients as experts in their own bodies.
- **Examine your own biases** about disability and quality of life.
- **Build relationships** with disability community organizations.
- **Advocate for systemic change** in healthcare that creates barriers for disabled patients.

For Workplace Leaders:

- **Recruit disabled employees** actively, not just when they apply.
- **Remove barriers** in job descriptions, application processes, and interview formats.
- **Provide flexibility** in work arrangements, schedules, and methods.
- **Create inclusive culture** where disability is valued, not just tolerated.
- **Ensure physical and digital accessibility** of all workplace systems and spaces.
- **Include disabled people** in leadership and decision-making positions.

- **Train all staff** on disability etiquette, accessibility, and inclusive practices.

For Everyone:

- **Use respectful language** based on individual preference.
- **Challenge exclusionary attitudes toward disability** when you encounter: in jokes, assumptions, media representation, or policies.
- **Make your own spaces accessible** whether that's your home, workplace, or events you organize.
- **Amplify disabled voices** by sharing their work, inviting them to speak, and deferring to their expertise.
- **Support disability-led organizations** through funding, volunteering, or partnerships.
- **Vote for accessibility** by supporting candidates and policies that prioritize disability rights.
- **Educate yourself** about disability history, culture, and current issues.
- **Practice humility** by acknowledging what you don't know and being open to correction.

Respectful Language Quick Reference:

DO: Ask people their preference for how they'd like to be described.

DO: Use "disabled person" or "person with a disability" based on individual preference.

DO: Say "wheelchair user" or "uses a wheelchair."

DO: Say "accessible" parking, bathroom, or entrance.

DON'T: Use "handicapped," "crippled," "invalid," or "special needs."

DON'T: Say "wheelchair-bound" or "confined to a wheelchair."

DON'T: Say "suffers from" or "victim of" when describing someone's disability.

DON'T: Say "normal" or "healthy" to mean non-disabled.

DON'T: Use disability as a metaphor for negative things ("that's so lame," "turn a blind eye," "falls on deaf ears").

Key Takeaway:

Communication is care.

When you slow down, ask clearly, listen deeply, and honor access needs, you transform communication from a transaction into a relationship. Respectful language isn't just semantics; it's a way of telling someone, "You matter, and I'm here with you."

Inclusion begins with how we speak, plan, and listen, not with the ramp at the door. True inclusion doesn't mean making room for disabled people in systems designed without us. It means redesigning systems with us from the beginning. When we shift from charity to justice, from tolerance to respect, from awareness to action, we create environments where everyone can participate fully.

Partnership, not pity, is the foundation of a just society. And every decision we make from here on determines whether we reinforce old systems or help build the inclusive future we all deserve.

PART VI
Digital Freedom and the Future

CHAPTER 11

DIGITAL AGE FREEDOM

The Screen as Equalizer

My community once thought becoming narrow had widened through the screen I now meet, see and talk to people from all over the world. We connect through different time zones and across oceans.

Thoughts, ideas, and contributions were evaluated on their merit, not filtered through assumptions about the body.

This was revolutionary.

Understanding how digital environments can level the playing field for disabled people in ways the physical world rarely does.

The digital space offered something profound: the choice of when and how to disclose disability, the freedom to be known for my capabilities before people encountered my limitations, the opportunity to build credibility before facing prejudice.

The Mentorship Network

Mentorship became a form of digital access in itself, an avenue where knowledge, confidence, and opportunity could travel freely across distance, barriers, and inequity.

Young disabled people discovering entrepreneurship. Parents of disabled children seeking guidance. College students with disabilities navigating career choices. Other disabled entrepreneurs building their own ventures.

These mentorship relationships remind us that digital access is disability access. When we remove physical barriers to connection, we create opportunities for people who've been systematically excluded.

Today's parents are raising children who will grow up digital. Technology can become their equalizer, not their barrier if we teach them early how to leverage its possibilities and advocate for its accessibility.

The Paradox of Digital Access

Hidden Barriers in Digital Spaces

But I want to be honest about something: digital spaces are not inherently equal. The same forces that gatekeep physical access often replicate themselves online through inaccessible platforms, poor design choices, and assumptions about who the "default" user is. These barriers are quieter, but they are no less real.

Economic and Access Inequity

Digital participation also requires reliable technology, high-speed internet, and the financial means to maintain both. Many people, disabled or not, are shut out long before they have the chance to benefit from the equality the internet can offer. Accessibility without affordability is not true access.

What I've Done in My Own Work

I've worked to address this in my own organizations and platforms. Reminding groups and businesses that all platforms must be accessible. Ensuring screen-reader compatibility, multiple communication formats, captioned content, and asynchronous options that honor people's processing needs. I've built systems meant to invite people in, not inadvertently leave them out.

Why Individual Action Isn't Enough

But individual efforts aren't enough. A just digital world requires responsibility, platforms that prioritize accessibility, institutions that remove financial barriers, and cultures that see access not as an accommodation but as a standard. Digital freedom cannot rely on personal heroics; it must be structurally guaranteed.

Website Accessibility:

- Screen-reader compatible design.
- Keyboard navigation throughout.
- High color contrast and adjustable text size.
- Alt text for all images.
- Captions and transcripts for all video content.

Virtual Event Accessibility:

- Captioning for all video calls.
- Materials shared in advance in multiple formats.
- Recording available for those who can't attend live.
- Breaks scheduled for fatigue management.
- Multiple participation options (video, audio, chat).

Economic Accessibility:

- Sliding scale pricing for services.
- Resources available for those who can't pay.
- Scholarships for workshops and programs.
- Consulting for disability-led organizations.

But individual efforts aren't enough. True digital freedom requires systemic change: platforms designed with accessibility from the start, internet access treated as a public utility, digital literacy education available to all.

The Fusion of Heart and Innovation

One concept that emerged from my digital work is what I call "heart-intelligence": the fusion of empathy (heart) with innovation (intelligence).

Heart-intelligence is the practice of pairing empathy with problem-solving, allowing innovation to be driven by lived experience rather than detached theory.

Technology is often framed as cold, rational, impersonal. But the most transformative technology emerges from deep understanding of human needs, from empathy with people facing barriers, from commitment to justice and inclusion.

Disabled innovators bring heart-intelligence naturally. We understand barriers intimately. We feel the frustration of exclusion personally. We're motivated not just by market opportunity but by lived experience of need.

This produces different and often better innovations:

Center lived experience. Prioritize insights from people who navigate barriers daily, not from distant observers or theoretical models.

Prioritize design that reduces harm. Innovation should make life easier, safer, and more dignified, not more complicated.

Measure impact by how people feel. Success is defined not just by efficiency, but by whether the outcome fosters trust, belonging, and ease.

Build solutions that grow with people. Heart-centered innovation evolves alongside the communities it serves, adapting as needs and contexts change.

The Purpose Question

As my digital businesses grew and my mentorship network expanded, I kept returning to one question: What's the purpose of all this?

Success, by conventional metrics, I'd achieved. Financial stability, professional recognition, impact on individuals' lives. These were real and meaningful.

But I wanted more than individual success. Digital freedom loses meaning if it only serves the few with resources and digital fluency. True equality requires that access pathways be built for everyone, not just those who manage to find them. I wanted systemic change. I wanted the digital freedom I'd experienced to be available to every disabled person, not just those with the resources and skills to access it.

This led to several initiatives:

Digital Literacy Programs: Free workshops teaching disabled people website creation, social media strategy, and online business basics.

Accessibility Consulting: Helping companies make their digital properties accessible, with fees from large clients subsidizing free services for small disability-led organizations.

Technology Access Fund: Providing grants for disabled entrepreneurs to purchase computers, software, and internet access needed to build digital businesses.

Mentorship Matching: Connecting experienced disabled digital professionals with those just starting, creating pipelines of knowledge transfer.

Advocacy Campaigns: Using digital platforms to push for stronger digital accessibility laws, better enforcement of existing standards, and platform accountability.

The purpose, I realized, wasn't just my own freedom. It was creating conditions for everyone's freedom, ensuring that the next generation of disabled people could access digital opportunities without facing the barriers I'd encountered.

Seeing The Whole Picture

From where I sit now in my home office, surrounded by adaptive technology, connected to a global network of disabled innovators and allies, I see possibility everywhere.

The teenager in rural India learning coding through free online courses, building skills that will lift her family out of poverty.

The disabled artist in Argentina selling work to collectors worldwide through digital galleries, no longer limited by local markets.

The disability advocate in Kenya organizing virtual workshops on accessibility, reaching audiences across the continent.

The autistic software developer in Canada working remotely for a company that values their skills, accommodates their needs, and respects their communication style.

These aren't hypotheticals. These are real people I've connected with, learned from, collaborated with, and celebrated with in digital spaces.

Technology hasn't solved all problems. Digital spaces still replicate many physical world barriers. Access remains unequal. But the potential is undeniable.

This is what digital age freedom means to me:

- Technology as a tool for independence, not a substitute for participation.
- Digital spaces as community connectors, not isolation chambers.
- Online platforms as amplifiers of marginalized voices, not just corporate megaphones.
- Innovation driven by empathy and justice, not just profit.
- Success measured in everyone's freedom, not just individual achievement.

The work continues. The challenges remain real. But from where I sit, digitally connected to a global community of disabled innovators, advocates, and dreamers, I can see the freedom we're building together.

It's not a future where technology fixes disability; disability doesn't need fixing. It's a future where technology removes barriers, where digital tools enable participation, where online communities provide support, and where disabled people lead the innovation that transforms our shared world.

That future is already arriving. We're building it right now, one accessible website at a time, one online community at a time, one digital business at a time, one act of heart-intelligence at a time.

Digital freedom is not simply a technological shift; it is a human one, shaped by connection, access, and the ingenuity of disabled people leading the way.

And from where I sit, the view of that future is spectacular.

CHAPTER 12

BUILDING INCLUSIVE FUTURES THROUGH TECHNOLOGY

Technology has always been a double-edged sword for disabled people. On one hand, innovations like wheelchairs, screen readers, and communication devices have transformed lives. On the other hand, technologies designed without accessibility in mind create new barriers, excluding disabled people from essential services, employment, and social participation.

But we stand at a unique moment: emerging technologies, artificial intelligence, remote work infrastructure, universal design platforms, offer unprecedented opportunities to build genuinely accessible futures. The question is whether these technologies will be designed with disabled people or imposed upon us, whether they'll remove barriers or create new ones, whether they'll be tools of freedom or instruments of further marginalization.

At the center of all of this is one truth: inclusive futures will only emerge if disabled people are not just consulted, but positioned as designers, engineers, founders, and decision-makers shaping the next generation of technology.

The answer depends on who's building the future and that's where disability-led innovation becomes essential.

Digital Entrepreneurship and Disability

Entrepreneurship has historically been challenging for disabled people. Traditional business models required physical storefronts (often inaccessible), in-person networking (exhausting or impossible for many disabled people), and access to capital (systematically denied to marginalized groups).

But digital entrepreneurship changes the equation.

Barriers Removed by Digital Business Models

Geographic Limitations: Digital work allows entrepreneurs to reach clients and collaborators regardless of location, eliminating reliance on inaccessible physical environments.

Physical Infrastructure Barriers: No need for brick-and-mortar storefronts, inaccessible workplaces, or transportation.

Lower Capital Requirements: Startup costs are significantly reduced, allowing disabled entrepreneurs to compete on equal footing with those who have greater financial access.

Flexible Schedules: Work can be done at variable energy levels, with rest integrated as needed supporting chronic illness, fatigue cycles, and diverse body/mind rhythms.

Remote Collaboration: Meetings, networking, and teamwork can occur asynchronously or through accessible platforms, reducing social and sensory barriers.

Self-Paced Workflow: Disabled entrepreneurs can work at the timing, speed, and pacing that align with their health and capacity, rather than conforming to rigid 9–5 expectations.

These shifts aren't just theoretical. Research now confirms what disabled entrepreneurs have long known: digital ecosystems open doors that traditional structures kept shut.

Research on Digital Entrepreneurship

Studies show that people with disabilities are more likely to be self-employed than non-disabled people, often out of necessity when traditional employment isn't accessible. Digital platforms have accelerated this trend.

Research on disabled entrepreneurs leveraging digital platforms found that they reported greater autonomy over work conditions, ability to compete on more equal footing with non-disabled competitors, access to markets that wouldn't have been available otherwise, and reduced discrimination compared to traditional employment.

Examples of Disability-Led Digital Innovation

Haben Girma, Disability Rights Lawyer and Consultant: Deafblind attorney who built a thriving consulting practice helping organizations improve digital accessibility. Her online presence and digital consulting model allow her to work with clients globally.

Tommy Edison, Blind Film Critic: Built a successful YouTube channel reviewing movies from a blind perspective, demonstrating that disability provides a unique valuable perspective, not limitation.

Tiffany Yu, Diversability Founder: Created an online platform connecting disabled people with resources, community, and employment opportunities. The digital model allows for global reach and accessibility built in from inception.

These entrepreneurs demonstrate that digital spaces offer opportunities not despite disability, but through the unique perspectives disability provides.

The Role of AI, Remote Work, and Universal Access

Three technological trends are converging to create unprecedented opportunities for disability access: artificial intelligence, remote work infrastructure, and universal access platforms.

Artificial Intelligence and Disability Access

AI offers both promises and perils for disabled people. Used thoughtfully, AI can remove barriers. Used carelessly, it can amplify discrimination.

Promising AI Applications:

- **Automated Captioning:** AI-powered speech-to-text makes video content accessible to deaf users. While not perfect, it's dramatically better than no captions.
- **Image Description:** AI can generate alt text for images, making visual content more accessible to blind users. Tools like Microsoft's Seeing AI and Google's Lookout use computer vision to describe surroundings.
- **Predictive Text and Voice Typing:** AI-powered text prediction helps people with motor disabilities or dyslexia communicate more easily.
- **Navigation Assistance:** AI-powered navigation apps help blind users navigate physical spaces, identifying obstacles and suggesting routes.
- **Translation:** AI translation makes content accessible across languages, benefiting deaf users who use sign language as a primary language.
- **Personalized Learning:** AI can adapt educational content to individual learning styles, benefiting neurodivergent learners and people with cognitive disabilities.

Concerning AI Risks:

- **Creates automated discrimination** when algorithms reproduce data biases related to race, disability, gender, or perceived normalcy.
- **Excludes users** when platforms rely on assumptions about sight, hearing, cognition, or mobility that do not reflect the reality of human bodies and minds.
- **Compromises privacy** when disability-related data is collected, stored, or shared without transparency or meaningful consent.
- **Increases vulnerability** when over-reliance on AI leads to gaps in critical human support especially when systems fail, glitch, or produce incorrect outputs.

The key is ensuring disabled people lead AI development so our needs and concerns shape technology from inception.

Remote Work Revolution

The COVID-19 pandemic forced a global experiment in remote work, proving what disabled workers had long argued: many jobs can be done remotely, and remote work benefits everyone.

For disabled workers, remote work offers:

Elimination of Commute Barriers: No need to navigate inaccessible public transportation or expensive accessible private transportation.

Accessible Home Environments: Workers can set up workspaces meeting their specific needs without requesting workplace modifications.

Flexible Schedules: Ability to work during high-energy periods and rest during low-energy periods, crucial for people with chronic illness or pain.

Reduced Discrimination: Less exposure to workplace microaggressions.

Energy Conservation: Energy that would be spent managing inaccessible environments can be directed to productive work.

Research shows that remote work increased employment rates for people with disabilities significantly. But remote work isn't automatically accessible. Digital inaccessibility can exclude disabled workers from remote opportunities just as physical inaccessibility excluded them from in-person work.

Universal Access Platforms

Universal access means designing digital platforms usable by people with diverse abilities from inception, not retrofitting accessibility afterward. These principles are strongest when shaped directly by disabled designers and engineers who understand access not as an afterthought but as the foundation of usability.

Principles of Universal Digital Access:

Perceivable: Information presented in ways users can perceive regardless of sensory abilities text alternatives for images, captions for audio, visual alternatives for audio-only content.

Operable: Interface usable regardless of input method keyboard navigation not requiring mouse, voice control options, adequate time to complete actions, no flashing content seizure risk.

Understandable: Content and interface comprehensible plain language, consistent navigation, error prevention and correction, predictable behavior.

Robust: Compatible with diverse assistive technologies semantic HTML, proper coding, testing with actual assistive technology, forward compatibility as technology evolves.

These principles provide a framework for building accessible digital experiences.

Technology Companies Leading on Accessibility

Microsoft: Has prioritized accessibility across products, from Xbox Adaptive Controller to AI-powered accessibility features in Office.

Apple: Built accessibility into operating systems with Voice Over, Switch Control, and other features standard on all devices.

Google: Developed accessibility features in Android, Chrome, and Google Workspace, often led by disabled engineers.

These companies demonstrate that accessibility can be good business, expanding markets, improving products for all users, and attracting talent.

The Fusion of Heart and Innovation

The most transformative technologies emerge when technical innovation is guided by deep empathy, understanding human needs, recognizing barriers, and designing for genuine inclusion.

This fusion, what I call "heart-intelligence," is where disabled innovators excel. We bring lived experience of exclusion, intimate understanding of barriers, and creativity born from constant adaptation.

Components of Heart-Intelligence

Empathetic Understanding: Deep comprehension of user needs based on lived experience or genuine listening to those with lived experience.

Human-Centered Design: Placing actual human needs, not theoretical features, at the center of innovation.

Justice Orientation: Understanding technology as a tool for equity, not just profit.

Sustainable Design: Creating solutions that respect human limitations and environmental constraints.

Community Accountability: Building with communities, not for them; being accountable to those you're serving.

Examples in Action

What Heart-Intelligence Looks Like in Practice

Be My Eyes: App connecting blind users with sighted volunteers for visual assistance. Founded by blind entrepreneur Hans Jørgen Wiberg based on his own need.

Wheelmap.org: Crowdsourced accessibility mapping platform created by disability advocates to help wheelchair users navigate cities.

The Deaf Professional Arts Network (D-PAN): Creates accessible music videos and arts content, innovating new ways to experience audio through visual and tactile elements.

Ava: Real-time captioning app founded by deaf entrepreneurs to make conversations accessible anywhere.

These innovations emerged from empathy rooted in lived experience. Disabled innovators didn't need market research to identify the problem; they lived it daily.

Building Accessible Futures: A Call to Action

The future isn't fixed. Technology can widen access or shut people out. What it becomes depends on the choices we make right now.

For Technology Companies:

- Hire disabled people across roles, especially in technical and leadership positions.
- Build accessibility into products from inception, not as an afterthought.
- Test with disabled users throughout development.
- Publish accessibility roadmaps and be accountable to them.
- Support open-source accessibility tools.
- Advocate for strong accessibility regulations.

For Policymakers:

- Strengthen and enforce digital accessibility laws.
- Require accessibility in government technology procurement.
- Fund digital literacy programs for disabled people.
- Support broadband access as a public utility.
- Ensure AI regulations address disability discrimination.
- Include disabled people in technology policy development.

For Educators:

- Integrate accessibility into computer science and design curricula.
- Teach disability history and disability justice.
- Provide accessible educational technology.
- Support disabled students pursuing technology careers.
- Partner with the disability community on research and innovation.

For Parents and Families:

- Introduce children to technology early as a tool for independence.
- Teach digital literacy alongside traditional literacy.
- Connect children with disabled technologists as role models.
- Encourage exploration and innovation.
- Advocate for accessible technology in schools.

For Disabled People:

- Claim space in technology fields; your expertise is needed.
- Build the tools you need; others need them too.
- Share knowledge and support other disabled innovators.
- Demand accessibility; you deserve it.
- Lead the future you want to see.

For Allies:

- Amplify disabled voices in technology discussions.
- Challenge inaccessibility when you encounter it.
- Learn about accessibility and integrate it into your work.
- Support disability-led technology initiatives.
- Use your influence to open doors for disabled technologists.

Toolkit: Supporting Technology Independence

Understanding the promise of accessible technology is powerful but putting it into practice is what transforms possibility into lived freedom. This toolkit gives you concrete ways to support children, students, and young adults as they grow into confident, capable digital citizens and future innovators.

What You Can Do Right Now:

These immediate steps help integrate technology as a tool of empowerment, not an exception, not a burden, and not something a young person has to "earn".

Introduce assistive technology early and without hesitation. Frame Assistive Technology (AT) as a tool like glasses or pencils, not a sign of limitation. Present it as something that expands what a young person *can* do, not something meant to "fix" them.

Let young people explore multiple tech tools to find what fits. Offer options: different Augmentative and Alternative Communication (AAC) apps, various navigation tools, adjustable display settings, coding platforms with accessibility built-in. Choice builds agency.

Use child-friendly language that emphasizes usefulness, not deficit. Instead of "This helps because you can't read small print," try: "This tool makes text bigger so your eyes can relax."

Make personalization part of the process. Allow customization, color schemes, icons, voices, stickers on devices, screen themes. Ownership increases comfort and confidence.

Model calm problem-solving when tech glitches happen. Your reaction becomes their internal script: "Technology sometimes hiccups. We can troubleshoot this together."

Connect them with disabled technologists and creators. Representation matters. Seeing people who use AAC, screen readers, or adaptive devices modeling confidence transforms what children believe is possible.

Practice digital self-advocacy scripts. Help them rehearse responses like: "Captions help me follow along." or "I use this app because it makes things easier for me."

Make online safety a shared conversation. Teach privacy, consent, boundaries, and safe exiting strategies. Empowerment requires safety.

Celebrate tech-enabled successes. If they navigate somewhere independently using an app, complete homework with a screen reader, or use AAC in a new setting. Honor it. These are milestones.

Accessible Technology Tools by Need:

For communication:

- Text-to-speech and speech-to-text tools.
- Augmentative and alternative communication (AAC) apps.
- Video calling with captions.

For learning:

- Audiobooks and text-to-speech readers.
- Adjustable text size and color contrast.
- Educational apps with multiple input methods.

For organization:

- Visual schedules and timers.
- Task management apps with reminders.
- Calendar apps with multiple alert types.

For creativity:

- Accessible drawing and design tools.
- Music creation apps with various input methods.
- Video editing with keyboard navigation.

For independence:

- Navigation apps with accessibility features.
- Money management apps with voiceover.
- Transportation apps showing accessibility info.

Daily Habits That Help:

Tech empowerment doesn't grow from big moments, it grows from predictable, nurturing routines that affirm capability.

Ask daily check-in questions about comfort and usability.

“What’s working well today?”

“What feels annoying or tiring?”

This builds self-awareness and trust.

Normalize troubleshooting as part of life.

Restarting apps, adjusting settings, or switching to a backup tool shouldn’t feel like failure; they’re signs of digital maturity.

Encourage experimentation.

Let them try new features or tools, even if they seem advanced. Exploration builds adaptability, creativity, and confidence.

Use affirming, specific praise.

“Your solution to that glitch was brilliant.”

Or

“You figured out a new way to navigate that app; love your creativity!”

Treat technology breaks as healthy, not punitive.

Rest is regulation. Disabled children especially may need pauses to reset energy, focus, or sensory load.

End the day with a moment of tech reflection.

“What did technology help you do today?”

This reinforces independence and agency.

What to Watch For:

Most young people need time to get comfortable with new tools. Some frustration is natural. But when specific patterns linger or intensify, it may signal the need for additional support; technical, emotional, or both.

- **Avoidance or refusal to use certain tools** → May indicate overwhelm, shame messaging, or frustration with inaccessible design.
- **Statements that express inadequacy or embarrassment** → "I don't want people to see this," "I look weird," or "I hate my device" can be early signs of stigma internalization.
- **Physical fatigue after device use** → Could suggest poor ergonomics, sensory overload, or overly complex interfaces.
- **Increasing reliance on one tool despite more effective options being available** → May signal fear of being visible or a desire to "pass."
- **Social withdrawal in online or offline spaces** → Could be connected to inaccessible platforms, online hostility, or tech anxiety.
- **Frustration out of proportion to the task** → Sometimes caused by small, fixable accessibility barriers (button size, layout, contrast).
- **Anxiety around data privacy or unfamiliar platforms** → Indicates the need for more transparent explanation and guided experience.

If you notice these patterns, respond with curiosity, not correction. Ask open-ended questions, involve them in problem-solving, and collaborate with teachers, therapists, or tech professionals when needed. Remember: resistance is often a form of communication, not defiance.

How to Keep Perspective:

Technology is powerful, but it is not magic and it is not linear. Some days your child will navigate the digital world with exhilarating independence; other days, even simple tasks may feel draining.

Your steadiness becomes their anchor.

Approach the journey with these reminders:

- **You don't need to have all the answers.**
  Curiosity and willingness to learn matter more than perfect tech expertise.

- **Progress happens in waves.**
  Mastery often looks like "two steps forward, one step back." That is still growth.

- **Your emotional tone becomes their internal landscape.**
  When you greet technology challenges with patience and compassion, you teach resilience more powerfully than any app.

- **Community makes a difference.**
  Connect with other disabled families, tech mentors, and accessibility communities. Shared knowledge multiplies empowerment.

- **Innovation grows from accommodation.**
  When we empower disabled children to use tools that fit their bodies, brains, and energy, we are not "spoiling" them, we are cultivating tomorrow's inventors.

There is no perfect path. There is only the present moment, the child in front of you, and the tools you're learning to navigate together.

Teaching Digital Problem-Solving:

When technology doesn't work, teach troubleshooting: restart, check settings, try alternatives.

When accessibility features are missing, teach advocacy: how to request features, report barriers, suggest improvements.

When online spaces aren't welcoming, teach boundary-setting: how to leave uncomfortable situations, block/report, find supportive communities.

When children create workarounds, celebrate that innovation and help them document/share their solutions.

Key Takeaway:

Technology becomes transformative when it is framed not as modification but as freedom. When young people learn that digital tools expand their world, and that they deserve those tools, they gain a lifelong sense of possibility. Independence grows not from forcing adaptation but from honoring differences.

The future belongs to disabled innovators. When we give children the tools, affirmation, and representation they need, we don't just build digital literacy, we help build accessible futures for everyone.

Your participation matters every decision you make, every barrier you challenge, and every innovation you support helps determine the kind of technological future the next generation will inherit.

CHAPTER 13

AGING WITH DISABILITY

When I was younger, transitioning between devices, navigating inaccessible buildings, and fighting for my place in a world that did not expect me, I had fire. I had energy. I had a body that, while different, still responded when I asked it to do hard things.

I had already learned how to adapt.

I thought that was enough.

What I did not fully anticipate was this next transition: aging with disability.

And I am realizing now that no one prepared me for it.

The Friends Who Didn't Make It

Over the past few years, I have watched friends with disabilities die in their fifties. Not from accidents. Not from sudden tragedy. From the cumulative toll of living in bodies that worked harder, endured more, and received less support than they deserved.

One was a close friend who led a major disability rights organization. A quadriplegic. A fierce advocate. Someone who fought alongside me for accessibility, recognition, and change. He died in his fifties. I believed we would grow old together, trading stories about the battles we fought and the progress we helped shape.

Another was one of the top attorneys in Chicago. Also a quadriplegic. Brilliant. Relentless. I had written to him not long before he passed, reminiscing about the work we had done. When I learned he was gone, the ground shifted beneath me. Another voice silenced. Another future erased.

Then there was the architect. A man who worked with major corporations to redesign spaces for accessibility. Gone as well. Also in his fifties.

These were not fragile people.

They were warriors.

But bodies have limits. Even determination cannot override them forever.

Learning to Age Without Teachers

What strikes me most now is this: I do not have mentors for this stage of life.

The hardest part wasn't the physical change. It was having no one who understood.

No one to talk to about the fear, the anger, the grief. I processed it all internally, alone in my apartment, trying to figure out who I was going to be now.

There were no support groups. No mentors who had been through this. No disability community I knew how to find. Just me and this new reality, figuring it out one impossible day at a time.

When I was younger, I could look to others who had already navigated that transition. There were fewer than there should have been, but they existed.

Now, as I face aging with disability, I realize how rare it is to find someone who has lived long enough to teach me what comes next.

Most people with significant disabilities from my generation did not make it this far. Those who did are asking the same questions I am, without a guidebook, without a roadmap, without elders to lean on.

How do I age gracefully when my body is already compromised?

How do I adapt when the adaptations I have relied on for decades no longer work?

How do I maintain independence when my strength fades faster than it would in a non-disabled body?

The Shift to a Power Chair

My wrists hurt.

My shoulders ache in ways they did not ten years ago.

For decades, I propelled myself in a manual wheelchair. It was freedom. It was autonomy. It was my red declaration of independence.

But repetitive motion has a cost. Years of pushing, lifting, compensating, and proving myself have caught up with me. My joints are not weak. They are worn. Overused. Exhausted.

So I am making another transition.

To a power chair.

This decision surprised me with its emotional weight.

I felt grief and relief at the same time. Frustration and acceptance tangled together. It felt like another loss of control, even though I knew the truth: this choice preserves energy, mobility, and longevity.

That is the complicated reality of disability. Sometimes the tools that give us freedom also feel like markers of decline. But decline is not the right word.

This is strategy.

This is survival.

This is wisdom earned the hard way.

A Body Aging Faster Than Expected

Aging with disability is not the same as aging without it.

Non-disabled people expect certain changes as they grow older. Less stamina. Aching joints. A gradual slowing.

For those of us who have lived with disability for decades, the process is different. The decline comes faster, hits harder, and behaves unpredictably.

My body is not failing catastrophically. It is shutting down quietly. Incrementally. In ways that remind me this body has been working overtime for more than fifty years.

Many healthcare professionals do not understand this distinction. They treat aging with disability as typical aging. It is not.

A sixty-year-old wheelchair user may have the musculoskeletal wear of someone fifteen years older. Compensatory movement patterns take a toll. Overuse injuries accumulate. Pain becomes layered rather than episodic.

We need doctors who understand this reality.

We need medical systems that recognize long-term disability as a distinct aging trajectory.

We need research, resources, and real solutions, not platitudes about "staying positive."

The Mental and Emotional Weight

The hardest part is not physical.

It is the mental and emotional labor of staying engaged, staying hopeful, staying present in a body that keeps asking me to let go of things I once took for granted.

There is a pull toward depression that I actively resist. Not because I am weak, but because loss is real. Watching friends die young is real. Feeling your body betray you again is real.

I have spent my life refusing to be defined by limitations. Now I must reckon with new ones.

The work is not pretending they do not exist.

The work is adapting again without losing myself.

I remind myself that I have done this before. I chose a wheelchair when walking became impossible. I built a career when the world said disabled people did not belong in professional spaces. I advocated for access when no one wanted to listen.

I can do this too.

But it is hard.

And I do not have all the answers.

What I Want Healthcare Professionals to Understand

If you work with people who have disabilities, please hear this clearly:

Aging with disability is not the same as typical aging.

Our bodies have been compensating for decades. We have expended more energy to accomplish the same tasks. That cost accumulates.

We need:

- Medical professionals trained in long-term disability aging trajectories.
- Research on how conditions progress differently in disabled bodies.
- Access to adaptive equipment that evolves as we age.
- Mental health support that acknowledges grief without pathologizing it.
- Communities where aging disabled people can learn from one another.

See us as whole people navigating an under-researched, under-supported stage of life.

What I Want Younger Disabled People to Know

You grew up with the ADA.

You saw disabled people in media, leadership, and public life.

That progress matters. We fought for it.

But do not take it for granted.

Do not become dormant.

Do not fall asleep at the wheel.

Rights are fragile. They require vigilance, advocacy, and resistance to erasure.

Fight.

But also be kind to yourselves.

Aging with disability will come for you too. When it does, I hope you will have mentors, resources, and systems that I am still searching for.

I hope you will not have to figure it out alone.

The Road Ahead

I do not know what the next decade holds. I do not know how my body will change or what new adaptations I will need.

But I know this: I am still here.

The red wheelchair may become a power chair, but it is still mine. Still my declaration of presence in a world that too often overlooks people like me.

I am aging.

I am changing.

I am facing losses I did not expect.

But I am not disappearing.

I remain visible.

I remain engaged.

I remain unwilling to let anyone else define who I am.

As long as I am here, I will keep rolling forward. However that looks. Whatever it takes.

Because that is what I have always done.

And that is what I will keep doing, until the road runs out.

EPILOGUE

THE MOMENT WE'RE IN

From where I sit today in my power chair, in my home office, surrounded by decades of adaptive equipment that tells the story of my journey, I can finally see what I couldn't as a child in Ecuador, a teenager on crutches, or a young professional resisting the wheelchair that would one day free me.

I can see that everything I thought was limitation was actually preparation.

The Journey in Review

The leg braces taught me adaptation before I had words for it. They showed me that my body would always work differently, that "normal" wasn't the goal, and that survival required creativity. They introduced me to the concept that equipment could be both a burden and a blessing, both a visible marker of difference and a tool for function.

The crutches helped me with energy management, strategic thinking, and with seeing the exhausting reality of visible disability in a world that treats difference as deficiency. I learned that some pain is unavoidable, but that persistence is possible. I was able to plan, to innovate, to find alternatives when standard paths were blocked.

I discovered visibility and reclamation because of the cane. I could transform symbols of stigma into expressions of style, refuse the mandate to minimize my difference, and claim space and demand respect. Professional success and disability weren't contradictory, even when others assumed they were.

The wheelchair oh, the wheelchair taught me everything. Like that freedom sometimes looks like surrender, that accepting reality is more powerful than resisting it, that community exists in unexpected places. It showed me that independence and interdependence aren't opposites, that asking for help isn't weakness, that access is a right, not a privilege.

But more than anything, each device helped me to see differently.

Seeing Differently

Before disability consciousness, I saw stairs as the natural way to change elevations.

Now I see them as design choices that exclude.

Before, I saw narrow doorways as standard architecture.

Now I see them as barriers that could easily be designed wider.

These were the architectural lessons, the moments when I realized my environment wasn't neutral, but designed with assumptions that didn't include me.

Before, I saw my exhaustion as a personal failure.

Now I see it as the predictable result of navigating environments designed without considering my needs.

Before, I saw disability as an individual tragedy.

Now I see it as a social category shaped by policy, design, and attitude.

And these were the internal lessons, the ones that shifted my understanding of myself, my body, and the systems shaping my daily life.

They also revealed something crucial: most people still see the old way. They see wheelchairs as tragic, accommodation as charitable, and disability as a problem requiring a solution. They see individuals who need fixing rather than systems that need changing.

The invitation of this book is to see differently to understand that:

- Disability is human diversity, not a medical emergency.
- Access is a justice issue, not a generous gift.
- Universal design benefits everyone, not just disabled people.
- Disabled people are experts whose knowledge should be valued and compensated.
- Inclusion requires redesigning systems, not just accommodating individuals.
- The barriers aren't in our bodies; they're in environments, attitudes, and policies.

Once you see it this way, you can't unsee it. And once you see, you become responsible for action.

Designing Differently

Seeing differently leads to designing differently.

If stairs exclude, design ramps and elevators from the beginning.

If standard keyboards create barriers, design alternative input methods.

If typical work schedules exhaust some workers, design flexibility.

If traditional education fails some learners, design multiple means of engagement, representation, and expression.

If physical spaces exclude, design universal access.

If digital platforms create barriers, design for accessibility from inception.

This isn't complicated. It's not prohibitively expensive. It's not impossible. Most of the time, accessibility simply requires shifts in priorities, not massive budgets.

Universal design becomes actionable when we commit to practices like these:

1. **Including disabled people in design processes.** Not as an afterthought or token representation, but as equal partners with decision-making power.
2. Asking "Who does this exclude?" at every stage. Making exclusion visible and unacceptable.
3. **Designing for diversity from the start.** Recognizing that one-size-fits-all never actually fits all.
4. **Testing with actual disabled users.** Not assuming what will work, but learning from those with lived experience.
5. **Iterating based on feedback.** Understanding that accessibility is an ongoing commitment, not a one-time achievement.
6. **Measuring participation, not just compliance.** Evaluating success by inclusion and satisfaction, not just legal minimums.
7. **Celebrating disability culture.** Recognizing disability as identity and community, not just a medical category.

When we design differently when we center margins, prioritize access, and value disability expertise, we don't just create accommodations for disabled people. We create innovations that benefit everyone.

The curb cuts designed for wheelchairs help parents with strollers, travelers with luggage, delivery workers, cyclists, and elderly people. The captions created for deaf users help language learners, people in noisy environments, and anyone who processes information better through reading than listening. The flexible work arrangements requested by disabled employees reduce burnout and increase satisfaction for all workers.

Universal design isn't charity. It's smart design that recognizes human diversity as natural and designs for it intentionally.

Leading Differently

Seeing differently and designing differently lead inevitably to leading differently.

Traditional leadership models valorize individualism over interdependence, invulnerability over authenticity, competition over collaboration, and speed over sustainability. But these models falter in a rapidly changing world where complexity, unpredictability, and social inequity demand leaders who can listen deeply, adapt quickly, and design systems that work for more than the narrow few.

But disability experience teaches different leadership values:

Interdependence: Recognizing we all need support and that needing help doesn't diminish worth.

Authenticity: Leading from genuine experience rather than performing invulnerability.

Collaboration: Understanding that diverse perspectives create better solutions than homogeneous groupthink.

Sustainability: Respecting human limitations and building systems that work long-term.

Diversity: Valuing difference as strength and source of innovation.

These aren't just nice values. They're practical necessities in complex, rapidly changing environments where old models fail.

The leaders who will thrive in the future are those who can navigate ambiguity and constraint, center marginalized voices, design accessible systems, build authentic relationships, think systemically, innovate under pressure, and lead with empathy and justice.

These are precisely the skills disability experience develops.

This is why I say confidently: the best leaders are often those who've had to design their own path. Not because suffering builds character, but because navigating barriers develops capabilities that can't be taught in business school.

Disabled leaders bring empathy from experiencing marginalization, innovation from constant adaptation, strategic thinking from necessary planning, systems awareness from seeing exclusion, resilience from persistent barriers, creativity from constraint-driven problem-solving, and justice commitment from personal stakes in equity.

These aren't compensations for limitations. They're valuable capabilities that organizations desperately need.

The True Meaning of "Anything Is Possible"

The phrase "anything is possible" often appears in inspirational stories about disabled people, the implication being that if we just try hard enough, believe strongly enough, or inspire others sufficiently, we can overcome our disabilities and achieve the impossible.

But that's not what "anything is possible" means to me.

It doesn't mean disability can be overcome through willpower. It doesn't mean success is just about individual effort.

It means that when we remove barriers, environmental, attitudinal, systemic, disabled people can accomplish anything non-disabled people can, often in innovative ways.

I've designed shoes for people with hard-to-fit feet. I've founded a nonprofit working across continents. I've advocated for policy change. I've mentored hundreds of disabled people toward their goals. I've built accessible gardens where people gather and grow. I've created digital businesses that provide independence. I've spoken truth to power in rooms where I wasn't expected to belong.

Not because I'm exceptional. Because I had access to equipment, to education, to community, to technology, to opportunities. Because people invested in removing barriers.

"Anything is possible" isn't about individual heroism. It's about freedom.

The Invitation

This movement touches every part of society, so I want to speak directly to the different communities who shape and are shaped by disability.

If you're a disabled person, especially a young one just beginning this journey: You are not broken. Your body is not wrong. The barriers you face are real, but they're not inevitable. There is a community waiting for you. Your experience is expertise. Your difference is valuable. Your dreams are valid. And you deserve access, accommodation, and the opportunity to pursue whatever calls to you.

If you're a parent of a disabled child: Your child's disability is not a tragedy. Grieve the expectations you had, then build new dreams with your child, not for them. Center their voice, trust their experience, advocate fiercely for access, connect with the disability community, and raise them to be proud of who they are. The greatest gift you can give them is belief in their full humanity and capability.

If you're supporting a child who feels different, remember this: what they need most is not fixing; it's freedom, belonging, and belief. Freedom to be themselves. Belonging in communities that accept them. Belief that their lives have value and possibility exactly as they are.

If you're a healthcare professional: Your patients are whole people, not just diagnoses. Include children in conversations about their bodies. Ask adults about their goals, not just their symptoms. Understand that quality of life is defined by the person living it, not by medical metrics. Learn about disability culture. Examine your own assumptions about disability. And remember that your role is to support people's lives, not to normalize their bodies.

If you're an educator: Your disabled students are capable of learning, though they may learn differently. Design with accessibility from the start. Provide multiple means of engagement, representation, and expression. Hold high expectations while offering necessary supports. Include disability in the curriculum. Address misconceptions about disability when they arise. And remember that your most struggling student might be struggling with your pedagogy, not with their capacity.

If you're an employer, architect, policymaker, or designer: You have power to remove barriers or create them. Choose to build access into foundations. Hire disabled people and trust our expertise. Compensate lived experience. Exceed minimum standards. Test with actual users. Measure participation, not just compliance. And understand that designing for disability creates innovations benefiting everyone.

If you're an ally: Use your influence to open doors, amplify marginalized voices, and challenge systems. But remember that allyship isn't about speaking for disabled people; it's about facilitating our leadership. Listen more than you speak. Accept corrections gracefully. Do the work of education yourself rather than expecting disabled people to teach you. And commit to sustained action, not performative gestures.

If you're simply someone who wants to understand: Thank you for reading this far. Thank you for being willing to see differently. Now I invite you to act differently. Notice accessibility in your environment. Address language rooted in stereotypes about disability when you hear it. Support disability-led organizations. Vote for candidates who prioritize disability rights. Make your own spaces accessible. And understand that disability isn't separate from other humanitarian concerns; it intersects with race, gender, class, sexuality, and all aspects of identity.

The Current Viewpoint

From where I sit, and I do mean that literally, from this power chair that has given me more freedom than walking ever did, I can see the future we're building.

It's a future where ramps are standard, not exceptional. Where accessibility is assumed, not extraordinary. Where disabled people lead in every field. Where our expertise is valued and compensated. Where difference is celebrated, not stigmatized. Where access is justice, not charity. Where anything truly is possible because barriers have been removed.

That future isn't guaranteed. It's being built right now by disabled people refusing to accept exclusion, by allies, by innovators designing with empathy, by policymakers centering disability rights.

It's being built every time someone chooses a ramp over stairs, every time disabled voice is amplified, every time accessibility is prioritized, every time someone sees differently and acts on that new vision.

I've spent my life moving from one piece of equipment to another: braces to crutches to canes to wheelchairs. Each transition felt like loss at first, then revealed itself as transformation.

The pattern taught me that what looks like limitation often becomes freedom, that accepting reality opens possibilities that resisting it forecloses, that community is found in unexpected places, and that working toward change is both a burden and blessing.

From where I sit, I can see that my journey has been toward freedom. Not freedom from disability, but freedom to be fully ourselves, to pursue our dreams, to contribute our gifts, to lead our communities, to design our futures.

That's the view from here: possibility, freedom, and the unshakeable conviction that when we say "anything is possible," we mean it, not as inspiration, but as commitment to building the accessible world where it's true.

The view is magnificent. And it's clearer from where I sit than it ever was standing. Welcome to the view; now let's build the future we can finally see.

BIBLIOGRAPHY

American Institutes for Research. (2018). A hidden market: The purchasing power of working-age adults with disabilities. AIR.

Batson, C. D., Chang, J., Orr, R., & Rowland, J. (2002). Empathy, attitudes, and action: Can feeling for a member of a stigmatized group motivate one to help the group? Personality and Social Psychology Bulletin, 28(12), 1656-1666.

Batson, C. D., Lishner, D. A., & Stocks, E. L. (2015). The empathy-altruism hypothesis. In D. A. Schroeder & W. G. Graziano (Eds.), The Oxford handbook of prosocial behavior (pp. 259-281). Oxford University Press.

CAST. (2018). Universal Design for Learning guidelines version 2.2. Retrieved from http://udlguidelines.cast.org

Darling, R. B. (2013). Disability and identity: Negotiating self in a changing society. Lynne Rienner Publishers.

Diamond, A. (2013). Executive functions. Annual Review of Psychology, 64, 135-168.

Diamond, K. E., & Hong, S. Y. (2010). Young children's decisions to include peers with physical disabilities in play. Journal of Early Intervention, 32(3), 163-177.

Erikson, E. H. (1950). Childhood and society. W. W. Norton & Company.

Favazza, P. C., & Odom, S. L. (1997). Promoting positive attitudes of kindergarten-age children toward people with disabilities. Exceptional Children, 63(3), 405-418.

Forbes-Bell, S. (2025). Big dress energy: How fashion psychology can transform your wardrobe and your confidence. Piatkus.

Garland-Thomson, R. (1997). Extraordinary bodies: Figuring physical disability in American culture and literature. Columbia University Press.

Garland-Thomson, R. (2009). Staring: How we look. Oxford University Press.

George, B., Sims, P., McLean, A. N., & Mayer, D. (2007). Discovering your authentic leadership. Harvard Business Review, 85(2), 129-138.

Gibson, B. E., Teachman, G., Wright, V., Fehlings, D., Young, N. L., & McKeever, P. (2012). Children's and parents' beliefs regarding the value of walking: Rehabilitation implications for children with cerebral palsy. National Institutes of Health.

Gill, C. J. (1997). Four types of integration in disability identity development. Journal of Vocational Rehabilitation, 9(1), 39-46.

Girma, H. (2019). Haben: The Deafblind woman who conquered Harvard Law. Twelve.

Goffman, E. (1963). Stigma: Notes on the management of spoiled identity. Prentice-Hall.

Goleman, D. (1995). Emotional intelligence: Why it can matter more than IQ. Bantam Books.

Goleman, D. (1998). What makes a leader? Harvard Business Review, 76(6), 93-102.

Jackson, P. W. (1968). Life in classrooms. Holt, Rinehart & Winston.

Jason, L. A., Corradi, K., Torres-Harding, S., Taylor, R. R., & King, C. (2005). Chronic fatigue syndrome: The need for subtypes. Neuropsychology Review, 15(1), 29-58.

Kaye, H. S., Jans, L. H., & Jones, E. C. (2011). Why don't employers hire and retain workers with disabilities? Journal of Occupational Rehabilitation, 21(4), 526-536.

King, G., Law, M., King, S., Rosenbaum, P., Kertoy, M. K., & Young, N. L. (2003). A conceptual model of the factors affecting the recreation and leisure participation of children with disabilities. Physical & Occupational Therapy in Pediatrics, 23(1), 63-90.

LaPlante, M. P., & Kaye, H. S. (2010). Demographics and trends in wheeled mobility equipment use and accessibility in the community. Assistive Technology, 22(1), 3-17.

Liedtka, J. M. (1998). Strategic thinking: Can it be taught? Long Range Planning, 31(1), 120-129.

Linton, S. (1998). Claiming disability: Knowledge and identity. NYU Press.

Longmore, P. K. (2003). Why I burned my book and other essays on disability. Temple University Press.

Mace, R. L., Hardie, G. J., & Place, J. P. (1996). Accessible environments: Toward universal design. Center for Universal Design, North Carolina State University.

Marshak, L. E., Van Wieren, T., Ferrell, D. R., Swiss, L., & Dugan, C. (2010). Exploring barriers to college student use of disability services and accommodations. Journal of Postsecondary Education and Disability, 22(3), 151-165.

Martin, M. M., & Rubin, R. B. (1995). A new measure of cognitive flexibility. Psychological Reports, 76(2), 623-626.

Nario-Redmond, M. R., Kemerling, A. A., & Silverman, A. (2019). Hostile, benevolent, and ambivalent ableism: Contemporary manifestations. Journal of Social Issues, 75(3), 726-756.

Oliver, M. (1990). The politics of disablement. Macmillan.

Page, S. E. (2007). The difference: How the power of representation creates better groups, firms, schools, and societies. Princeton University Press.

Partnership on Employment & Accessible Technology (PEAT). (2021). The impact of COVID-19 on people with disabilities in the workplace. PEAT.

Roni, M., & Schur, L. (2017). Self-employment among people with disabilities: Evidence from the American Community Survey. Kauffman Foundation.

Rose, C. A., & Gage, N. A. (2017). Exploring the involvement of bullying among students with disabilities over time. Exceptional Children, 83(3), 298-314.

Rosenbaum, P., King, S., Law, M., King, G., & Evans, J. (1998). Family-centred service: A conceptual framework and research review. Physical & Occupational Therapy in Pediatrics, 18(1), 1-20.

Senge, P. M. (1990). The fifth discipline: The art and practice of the learning organization. Doubleday.

Sternberg, R. J. (1985). Beyond IQ: A triarchic theory of human intelligence. Cambridge University Press.

Stokes, P. D. (2006). Creativity from constraints: The psychology of breakthrough. Springer.

Story, M. F., Mueller, J. L., & Mace, R. L. (1998). The universal design file: Designing for people of all ages and abilities. North Carolina State University, Center for Universal Design.

Waters, R. L., Lunsford, B. R., Perry, J., & Byrd, R. (1988). Energy-speed relationship of walking: Standard tables. Journal of Orthopaedic Research, 6(2), 215-222.

Web Accessibility Initiative (W3C). (2018). Web Content Accessibility Guidelines (WCAG) 2.1. Retrieved from https://www.w3.org/WAI/WCAG21/quickref/

Weick, K. E., & Sutcliffe, K. M. (2007). Managing the unexpected: Resilient performance in an age of uncertainty (2nd ed.). Jossey-Bass.

Whittaker, M., Crawford, K., Dobbe, R., Fried, G., Kaziunas, E., Mathur, V., West, S. M., & Richardson, R. (2018). AI Now Report 2018. AI Now Institute at New York University.

World Health Organization. (2001). International classification of functioning, disability and health (ICF). WHO.

Young, S. (2012). We're not here for your inspiration. The Drum, ABC News. Retrieved from https://www.abc.net.au/news/2012-07-03/young-inspiration-porn/4107006

Young, S. (2014). I'm not your inspiration, thank you very much [Video]. TED Conferences. Young, S. (2014). I'm not your inspiration, thank you very much [Video]. TED Conferences.

Additional Resources for Readers

- www.EyesOnSuccess.net

Disability Rights Organizations:

- National Council on Independent Living (NCIL): www.ncil.org
- ADAPT: www.adapt.org
- Autistic Self Advocacy Network (ASAN): www.autisticadvocacy.org
- National Federation of the Blind (NFB): www.nfb.org
- National Association of the Deaf (NAD): www.nad.org
- American Association of People with Disabilities (AAPD): www.aapd.com

Disability Culture and Media:

- Disability Visibility Project: www.disabilityvisibilityproject.com
- Rooted in Rights: www.rootedinrights.org
- The Accessible Stall Podcast.
- Disability After Dark Podcast.

Universal Design Resources:

- Center for Universal Design: www.design.ncsu.edu/cud
- Institute for Human Centered Design: www.humancentereddesign.org
- Web Accessibility Initiative (WAI): www.w3.org/WAI

Disability-Led Organizations:

- Causes for Change International (causesforchange.org).
- Sins Invalid (disability justice performance project).
- The Disability Justice Collective.
- Harriet Tubman Collective.
- Partnership on Employment & Accessible Technology (PEAT).

Academic and Research Centers:

- Paul K. Longmore Institute on Disability (San Francisco State).
- Disability Studies Program at Syracuse University.
- Institute on Disability at University of New Hampshire.
- Burton Blatt Institute at Syracuse University.

Books for Further Reading:

- "Access Starts Here: How to Design Outdoor Spaces That Include, Inspire and Welcome Everyone" by Zully JF Alvarado.
- "Care Work: Dreaming Disability Justice" by Leah Lakshmi Piepzna-Samarasinha.
- "Being Heumann: An Unrepentant Memoir of a Disability Rights Activist" by Judith Heumann.
- "Disability Politics in a Global Economy" by Marta Russell.
- "The Pretty One: On Life, Pop Culture, Disability, and Other Reasons to Fall in Love with Me" by Keah Brown.
- "Demystifying Disability" by Emily Ladau.
- "Disability Studies: An Interdisciplinary Introduction" by Dan Goodley.

ABOUT THE AUTHOR

Zully JF Alvarado is an international speaker, entrepreneur, disability rights advocate, and founder of Causes for Change International. Born in Ecuador and brought to the United States for medical treatment as a child, she has spent her life transforming challenges into opportunities and barriers into bridges.

As a designer, she created innovative footwear for people with hard-to-fit feet, earning recognition in national magazines and winning multiple awards. As an advocate, she has led international missions providing health, education, and training services in underserved communities across Latin America.

As an entrepreneur, she now focuses on digital innovation and mentorship, helping others discover that technology can be a tool of freedom and that entrepreneurship can be a path to independence and impact.

Zully's work has been featured in major newspapers and magazines, and she has spoken to audiences around the world about disability rights, inclusive design, and the power of perspective.

She lives in Port Charlotte, Florida with her husband, where she continues to build bridges between ability and opportunity, between technology and humanity, and between individual dreams and collective change.

Connect With Zully

Want to follow Zully's work, upcoming projects, and advocacy efforts?

Scan the QR code to visit her Linktree where you can find her latest updates, social media, speaking information, and resources.

Visit accesszully.com or open your camera and scan.

www.ingramcontent.com/pod-product-compliance
Lightning Source LLC
LaVergne TN
LVHW020713110826
845149LV00012B/2248

* 9 7 9 8 9 9 9 3 9 8 8 5 7 *